It's another quality book from CGP...

Help is at hand for Grade 9-1 GCSE Religious Studies — this fantastic CGP book is perfectly tailored to Christianity, Catholic Christianity and Buddhism!

It's packed with crystal-clear study notes for the AQA A exam, plus plenty of exam-style questions to make sure you're ready for the real thing.

How to access your free Online Edition

This book includes a free Online Edition to read on your PC, Mac or tablet. To access it, just go to **cgpbooks.co.uk/extras** and enter this code...

2205 1519 9800 6435

By the way, this code only works for one person. If somebody else has used this book before you, they might have already claimed the Online Edition.

CGP — still the best! ☺

Our sole aim here at CGP is to produce the highest quality books — carefully written, immaculately presented and dangerously close to being funny.

Then we work our socks off to get them out to you — at the cheapest possible prices.

Contents

Theme C — The Existence of God and Revelation

Theme D — Religion, Peace and Conflict

Theme E — Religion, Crime and Punishment

Theme F — Religion, Human Rights and Social Justice

Theme G — St Mark's Gospel: the Life of Jesus

Theme H — St Mark's Gospel as a Source of Religious, Moral and Spiritual Truths

The green religion tags on the pages of each section tell you whether the page covers:

| Christianity | ...information about a specific religion... | Christianity & Buddhism | ...information about both religions... | General | ...or general information. |

Published by CGP

Editors: Robbie Driscoll, Daniel Fielding, Christopher Lindle, Sam Norman, Caroline Purvis

Contributors: Jill Hudson, Paul Smith, Lily Staff, Philip West

Reviewer: Alicia Sarbicki

Proofreading: Glenn Rogers, Paul Smith

ISBN: 978 1 78908 571 6

With thanks to Emily Smith for the copyright research.

Scripture quotations [marked NIV] taken from the Holy Bible,
New International Version Anglicised
Copyright © 1979, 1984, 2011 Biblica, Used by permission of Hodder & Stoughton Ltd, an Hachette UK company
All rights reserved
'NIV' is a registered trademark of Biblica
UK trademark number 1448790.

Quotations from the Catechism of the Catholic Church © Libreria Editrice Vaticana

Quotations used on pages 8, 14, 38 and 47 from The Church of England, https://www.churchofengland.org.
© The Archbishops' Council.

Quotations used on pages 30, 32, 33, 49, 53, 54, 75, 77 and 112 © Buddhist Publication Society, used by permission.

Quotations from Lumen gentium on page 16, Gaudium et spes on page 20, Evangelii Gaudium on pages 21 and 22,
Humanae Vitae on pages 39 and 52, Familiaris Consortio on pages 42, 43 and 45, and a speech by Pope Francis on page 47
© Libreria Editrice Vaticana

With thanks to Alamy for permission to use the images on page 13: Photo of Quaker meeting house © John Morrison / Alamy Stock
Photo, photo of evangelical church worship © Julio Etchart / Alamy Stock Photo and the image on page 52 © Isabelle Plasschaert /
Alamy Stock Photo.

With thanks to The Office of His Holiness the Dalai Lama to use the quotations on pages 33, 68, 82 and 84.

Source of statistic on belief in evolution on page 56: Theos

Image used on page 70 © iStock Editorial / Getty Images Plus / sadikgulec.

Data about wealth inequality on page 86 contains public sector information licensed under the Open Government Licence v3.0.
http://www.nationalarchives.gov.uk/doc/open-government-licence/version/3/

Every effort has been made to locate copyright holders and obtain permission to reproduce sources. For those sources where it has
been difficult to trace the originator of the work, we would be grateful for information. If any copyright holder would like us to
make an amendment to the acknowledgements, please notify us and we will gladly update the book at the next reprint. Thank you.

Printed by Elanders Ltd, Newcastle upon Tyne
Clipart from Corel®

Based on the classic CGP style created by Richard Parsons.

Introduction to Christianity

Christianity is based on the belief in **Jesus Christ** being the **Son of God**. It is the **main** religion in Britain.

The Bible is the Christian sacred text

The Bible is divided into two main parts — the **Old** and **New Testaments**:

OLD TESTAMENT

- Depending on the version, the **Old Testament** has at least 39 books, which include the **Creation** story (see p.4-5) and the **Ten Commandments**.
- These 39 books are the **Jewish scriptures** — they are also considered **sacred** by Jews.

NEW TESTAMENT

- The **New Testament** is the part of the Bible that is **specifically Christian**.
- Its 27 books include the **4 Gospels** (Matthew, Mark, Luke and John), which are accounts of **Jesus's life**.
- The **Acts of the Apostles** and the **letters of St Paul** describe the **early years** of Christianity.

Christianity is divided into different traditions

The different branches of Christianity are called **denominations**. They share key beliefs, but interpret some points of the faith differently and worship in different ways (see pages 12-13).

Roman Catholics

- **Roman Catholics** respect the authority of the **Bible** and **Church tradition**, plus the authority of the **Pope** and his teachings.
- The **seven sacraments** (which include the Eucharist — see p.14) are an important part of their faith.

Orthodox Christians

- **Orthodox Christians** are found mainly in Eastern Europe, Russia and Greece.
- They also have **7 sacraments**, and honour (but don't worship) **icons** — pictures of Saints.

Protestants

- **Protestants** base their beliefs and practices on the **Bible**, rather than Church tradition or the teachings of the Pope.
- In England and Wales, Protestant denominations that are not part of the 'Anglican Communion' are often called '**Nonconformists**'.

  These include Methodists, Baptists, Pentecostals, The Society of Friends (Quakers) and the Salvation Army.

The **Church of England** has both Roman Catholic and Protestant features. Its beliefs are set out in the **39 Articles**. **Anglicanism** is the worldwide 'communion' of Churches in fellowship with the parent Church of England.

EXAM TIP

The New Testament — not so new these days...

It's important to remember what a diverse range of traditions there is within Christianity. You need to know about contrasting religious beliefs for the exam, but that doesn't always mean writing about different religions — you can also compare Christian denominations too.

Introduction to Christianity

There are many beliefs about the nature of God

- Christianity is a **monotheistic** (one God) religion. The Ten Commandments say:

> **"You shall have no other gods"** *(Exodus 20:3 NIV)*

- Christians believe God has the following **characteristics**:

 **OMNIPOTENT**
God is **all-powerful**, although he still allows each person **free will**.

Christians differ in the emphasis placed on each characteristic, e.g. some focus more on God's loving nature than his role as judge.

 BENEVOLENT
God is **loving** and **caring**:

> **"For God so loved the world that he gave his one and only Son."** *John 3:16 NIV*

Christians try to **follow** his example in their actions.

 **JUST JUDGE**
- God **judges** people's actions fairly.
- Those who reject him and live sinful lives will be **punished**, as shown in the story of the sheep and goats in Matthew 25:31-46 (see p.22).
- But God **forgives** people who are sorry for what they've done and become faithful to him — the story of the **prodigal son** (Luke 15:11-32) shows God will forgive anyone who returns to his ways.

 ETERNAL
God has always existed, and he will continue to exist **forever**.

 **TRANSCENDENT**
God is **beyond** this world — he doesn't depend on it to exist.

 OMNISCIENT
God **knows** everything — in the past, present and future.

 **IMMANENT**
God is **present** in the human world, and takes an **active role** in humanity.

 **PERSONAL**
- God is a '**person**', albeit an almighty and **divine person**.
- If God is personal, then a relationship is possible through **prayer** — which can be a '**conversation**' with God.

REVISION TASK

Omnipotent or omniscient? Get them the right way round...

That might seem like an awful lot of characteristics, but it's important to know them all if you want to get a good idea of how Christians perceive God. So have a go at covering this page and seeing how many of them you can write down from memory. No peeking...

The Trinity

Although Christians believe in **one God**, they also believe that God has **three parts**.

Christians believe in God as the Trinity

The **Trinity** is the idea that God exists in three '**persons**' — the Father, the Son (Jesus) and the Holy Spirit. The **importance** of all three is shown in the Bible:

> "[Jesus] saw the Spirit of God descending like a dove and alighting on him. And a voice from heaven said, 'This is my Son, whom I love; with him I am well pleased.' " *Matthew 3:16-17 NIV*

This happened at Jesus's **baptism**.

> "[Jesus has] equality with God" *Philippians 2:6 NIV*

St Paul described Jesus this way.

The Trinity is explained in the Nicene Creed

In 325 AD, Church leaders from around the world gathered at the **Council of Nicaea**. They produced a **creed** — a statement of beliefs. This was further developed at the **Council of Constantinople** in 381 AD, and is known as the **Nicene Creed**. It describes how Christians see God:

> "We believe in one God, the Father, the Almighty, maker of heaven and earth... We believe in one Lord, Jesus Christ, the only Son of God... of one Being with the Father... was made man... he suffered death and... he rose again... We believe in the Holy Spirit... the giver of life, who proceeds from the Father and the Son... who has spoken through the prophets." *Nicene Creed*

- Before this, not everyone had **agreed** that the Son of God (Jesus) was **one with God**, rather than having been **made by God**. Now they agreed that he was **equally** important.
- The **importance** the **early Church** placed on the **Trinity** in the Nicene Creed means it is a **key belief** for most Christians — but some groups, such as **Christadelphians**, don't believe in the Trinity.
- Christians see the three parts of the Trinity as having **different characteristics** and **roles**:

For many Christians, **God the Father** is the God of the **Old Testament**. He **created** Heaven and Earth and **sustains** them. **God the Father** might be described as the **transcendent part** of God.

The title 'Father' is a mark of **respect** for God, and is used by **Jesus** in the Gospels:

> "Be perfect, therefore, as your heavenly Father is perfect." *Matthew 5:48 NIV*

Christians believe that the **Holy Spirit** is the **presence** of God in the world. Before his death, Jesus promised his disciples:

> "I will ask the Father, and he will give you another advocate to help you and be with you for ever — the Spirit of truth." *John 14:16-17 NIV*

Christians believe Jesus (see p.9-11) is the **incarnation** of God in human form. He is seen as both divine and human — the **immanent** and **personal** part of God, who understands human suffering.

Christians believe that Jesus provides a **model** for Christian behaviour in **obedience** to God the Father.

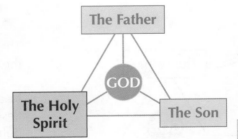

The Holy Spirit is seen as the **immanent yet impersonal** part of God — it continues to **guide** the **Church**.

Some Christians feel that the Holy Spirit also guides them **personally** in being good Christians.

> "By this power of the Spirit, God's children can bear much fruit." *Catechism of the Catholic Church 736*

The **Gospels** contain a record of his life and teachings, and are an important source of **guidance** for Christians on how they should live their lives.

EXAM TIP

Three into one doesn't go in maths — but this is RS...

For the 5 mark exam questions, you're going to have to refer to sacred texts. You can write quotes, or just paraphrase what is said. Say where it comes from, e.g. which book of the Bible.

Creation

The story of creation can be understood in different ways. Some take it **literally**, for others it's a **metaphor**.

The Bible describes how God created the universe

Genesis chapter 1 says that **God** created everything.
The process took **six days**, and on the seventh day God **rested**:

Day ①

Light and **darkness** were made.

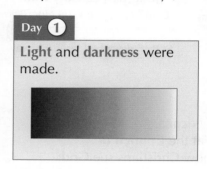

Day ②

The **sky** was made.

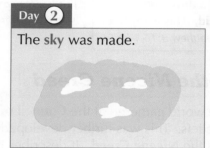

Day ③

Oceans, **land** and **plants** on the land were created.

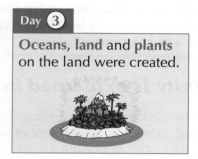

Day ④

The **sun**, **moon** and **stars** were created.

Day ⑤

The creatures of the water and sky (e.g. **fish** and **birds**) were created.

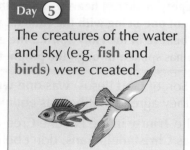

Day ⑥

Land animals and **people** were created.

Day ⑦

God rested.

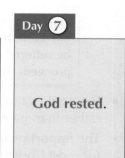

All the beings of the Holy Trinity were involved

Christians see God the Father as the **creator**.

The Father

The Holy Spirit

GOD

The Son

The role of the **Son of God** is described in the Gospel of John. He uses the phrase 'the Word', but it is clear he is referring to Jesus as he later says, *"The Word became flesh and made his dwelling among us"* (John 1:14 NIV). John makes it clear that Jesus was **vital for creation**.

"In the beginning was the Word, and the Word was with God, and the Word was God. He was with God in the beginning. Through him all things were made; without him nothing was made that has been made." *John 1:1-3 NIV*

God created the world by acting **through** the Holy Spirit.

"...the Spirit of God was hovering over the waters. And God said, 'Let there be light,' and there was light." *Genesis 1:2-3 NIV*

Creation

The Bible explains how human beings were created

The creation of human beings is described in **Genesis** chapters **1** and **2**.
The first two humans were **Adam and Eve**, and they lived in the **Garden of Eden**.

"So God created mankind in his own image, in the image of God he created them; male and female he created them." *Genesis 1:27 NIV*

"The Lord God formed a man from the dust of the ground." *Genesis 2:7 NIV*

"[God] made a woman from the rib he had taken out of man."*Genesis 2:7 NIV*

The fact that God created humans in **his image** is important:
- Because of this, Christians believe that humans are **special**. They think humans should **behave** like God by being **loving** and **fair** (see p.2).
- It also shows that humans are **important to God**, and so **everyone** should be treated with **respect**.

"Rule over the fish in the sea and the birds in the sky and over every living creature that moves on the ground." *Genesis 1:28 NIV*

God gave this instruction to Adam and Eve. Some Christians believe this means God gave humans '**dominion**' (power) over his creation and they can **use** it as they like.

"The Lord God took the man and put him in the Garden of Eden to work it and take care of it." *Genesis 2:15 NIV*

Many Christians interpret this as humans having '**stewardship**' of the Earth — God expects them to **care** for it.

There are different ways to interpret the creation story

Some Christians take the creation story literally...
- They are known as **creationists**.
- They believe that the process took six days, and humans are descended from Adam and Eve.

Other Christians are more liberal in their understanding of the Bible's events...
- They view Genesis as more of a **parable**, or a **symbolic** description.
- They acknowledge God as the creator, but are open to **other theories**, such as the **Big Bang theory** and **evolution**. These theories can offer more **information** to Christians about how **God** made the universe. The Roman Catholic Church has **accepted** both theories.

The creation story can help Christians further understand **God's nature**:

Eternal ⟹ God is **eternal** as he made time, and was present 'prior' to it.

Omnipotent ⟹ He is **omnipotent** as he created the universe through words.

Benevolent ⟹ God's **benevolence** can be seen through creation too as he brought humankind to life and gave them the world.

And you thought revision was tiring...

Grab a pen and paper and see if you can summarise what Genesis chapters 1 and 2 say about the creation. Once you've done that, try jotting down some different interpretations of creation.

Christianity	Evil and Suffering

Evil comes in **different forms**, and can have an **impact** on a person's relationship with their faith.

Free will led to evil entering the world

- **Christianity** teaches that evil **entered** the world as a result of **Adam and Eve** giving in to **temptation** in the Garden of Eden — they **disobeyed** God by eating the **fruit** of the tree of knowledge.

> **"When the woman saw... the fruit of the tree... she took some and ate it. She also gave some to her husband... and he ate it."** *Genesis 3:6 NIV*

'The Fall'
the switch from a perfect world to one containing evil after Adam and Eve disobeyed God

original sin
the idea that, after the Fall, every human being was born with a flawed nature, capable of causing suffering

- Christians believe God created humans with **free will**.
- It's up to humans to **choose** whether they perform evil deeds or not.
- This is shown in the story of **Adam and Eve** and how it was up to them whether to give in to temptation or not.
- **Good** is the opposite of **evil**, and since God is good, Christians try to follow his **example**.

Evil can be either human-made or natural

Evil and suffering can be divided into **two types**:

1 Moral (human-made) Evil

- This is when suffering is brought about by the **cruel** actions of **people**.
- This includes things like murder, war, rape and torture.
- The person causing the evil is able to make a **choice** about what is morally **right or wrong**.

2 Natural Evil

- This kind of evil, and the suffering that comes with it, is **caused by the world** in which we live, and is **no one's 'fault'**.
- This includes lots of things, but some examples include disease, floods, earthquakes and hurricanes.
- However, many **recent natural disasters** may have been caused by **human interference** in the natural world, raising the question of whether that makes those events human-made.

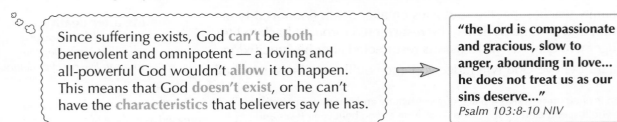

Evil and Suffering — Christianity

Evil can lead people to question their faith

- **Evil** and **suffering** may lead some people to **question** their belief in God — or even to **reject** their faith:

Since suffering exists, God **can't** be **both** benevolent and omnipotent — a loving and all-powerful God wouldn't **allow** it to happen. This means that God **doesn't exist**, or he can't have the **characteristics** that believers say he has.

"the Lord is compassionate and gracious, slow to anger, abounding in love... he does not treat us as our sins deserve..."
Psalm 103:8-10 NIV

- Christians **react** to the problem of evil and suffering in various ways:

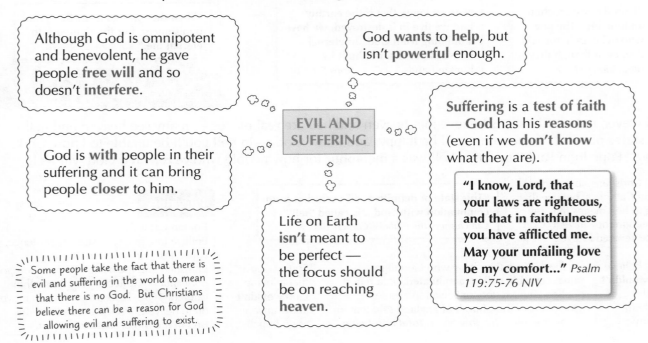

Although God is omnipotent and benevolent, he gave people **free will** and so doesn't **interfere**.

God **wants** to **help**, but isn't **powerful** enough.

God is **with** people in their suffering and it can bring people **closer** to him.

EVIL AND SUFFERING

Suffering is a **test of faith** — **God** has his **reasons** (even if we **don't know** what they are).

"I know, Lord, that your laws are righteous, and that in faithfulness you have afflicted me. May your unfailing love be my comfort..." *Psalm 119:75-76 NIV*

Life on Earth **isn't** meant to be perfect — the focus should be on reaching **heaven**.

Some people take the fact that there is evil and suffering in the world to mean that there is no God. But Christians believe there can be a reason for God allowing evil and suffering to exist.

The Book of Job teaches that suffering must be accepted

- The **Book of Job** tells of the **terrible suffering** Job endures and how he **questions** God. In the end, Job comes to the conclusion that God is **all-powerful** and knows what he is doing — and that suffering must be **accepted** because people can't really **understand** the world or **God's plan**.

"Though he slay me, yet will I hope in him..."
Job 13:15 NIV

- Christians believe they should try to **help** people who are suffering — **practically** (charity) and by **praying**. Jesus said that *"...whatever you did for one of... these brothers and sisters of mine, you did for me"* (Matthew 25:40 NIV).

Not the cheeriest of topics...

Christians explain and respond to evil and suffering in a variety of ways.
Cover this page, see how many you can think of and write them all down.

The Afterlife

What people believe will happen to them after **death** can influence the way they **live** their lives.

Christians believe in *heaven* and *hell*

- Christianity teaches that the **soul** lives on after death (**immortality** of the soul), and that the body will be **resurrected** (brought back to life) for Judgement Day, just as Jesus was resurrected after his crucifixion.

life after death
the idea that, although your body may die, your soul can live on after death

- Christians believe God will judge you and you'll go to **heaven** or **hell**:

Heaven is often portrayed as a place of great beauty and serenity, a **paradise** where you'll spend eternity with God — as long as you believe in **Jesus** and have followed his **teachings**, you can be saved by **God's grace** (see p.11). The **soul** can go to heaven even though the body ('earthly tent') is gone.

"I am the resurrection and the life. The one who believes in me will live, even though they die..." *John 11:25 NIV*

"For we know that if the earthly tent we live in is destroyed, we have a building from God, an eternal house in heaven, not built by human hands." *2 Corinthians 5:1 NIV*

Hell, on the other hand, is often portrayed as a place of **torment** and **pain** — the final destination of **nonbelievers** and those who have led **bad** lives.

"Then they will go away to eternal punishment, but the righteous to eternal life." *Matthew 25:46 NIV*

- However, not all Christians believe that heaven and hell are **real** places — many see heaven and hell as **states of mind**. In heaven you'll be **happy**, and know God — in hell you'll be **unable** to know God's love. Pope John Paul II said that hell was a **metaphor** for how people who've **rejected** God will **feel**.

Some Christians, for example Roman Catholics, believe that going to hell means that any **connection** they have to God will be **severed** forever.

"This state of definitive self-exclusion from communion with God... is called 'hell'" *Catechism of the Catholic Church 1033*

Read this if you're studying <u>Catholic Christianity</u>.

Purgatory

Roman Catholics believe in a place, or state of existence, called **Purgatory**. Here **sins** are punished and the person must *"undergo purification"* (Catechism of the Catholic Church, 1030) before the soul can move on to heaven. Protestants believe this isn't in the Bible, so they **reject** it.

Some believe God **wouldn't** punish people for **eternity**.

A few believe that those who God finds **unacceptable** will be **annihilated**. In a report called 'The Mystery of Salvation', senior members of the **Church of England** said that for those people *"the only end is **total non-being**"*.

Some believe that a loving God **wouldn't** allow anyone to go to hell.

Christians believe *resurrection* happens at the *Last Judgement*

- Many Christians believe that Jesus will return to Earth in the Second Coming (Parousia), and everyone who has died will be **resurrected**.

"Christ... ascended into Heaven, and there sitteth, until he return to judge all Men at the last day." *39 Articles IV*

- Some believe that all of humanity will then be judged at the Last Judgement. Those that God finds **acceptable** will enter **heaven** — the rest will go to hell, as in the story of the sheep and the goats (Matthew 25:31-46).

"in Christ all will be made alive" *1 Corinthians 15:22 NIV*

"For we must all appear before the judgement seat of Christ, so that each of us may receive what is due to us for the things done while in the body, whether good or bad." *2 Corinthians 5:10 NIV*

Some Christians, e.g. Roman Catholics, believe in a personal day of judgement straight after a person dies — their actions will be judged and they'll go to heaven or hell straight away.

Some think they'll be judged again at the Last Judgement, and will re-enter heaven or hell in their resurrected forms.

Others don't believe in a personal judgement — the soul must wait to be judged at the Last Judgement.

EXAM QUESTION

The examiners will be judging your answers...

Explain two Christian beliefs about judgement. Give examples to illustrate your answer. [5]

Jesus Christ and Salvation

Christians believe that Jesus Christ, the second Person of the Trinity, is the **Son of God**.

God became human at the incarnation

- The **incarnation** was the act by which **God** became a **human being** as Jesus Christ.
- An **angel** told a woman called **Mary** in Nazareth that she would have a **son** — and that *"the holy one to be born will be called the Son of God"* (Luke 1:35 NIV).

> *"he... was incarnate from the* **Holy Spirit and the Virgin Mary and was made man"** *Nicene Creed*

JESUS

- Christians don't believe that Jesus was 'half God and half man' — he was **fully both**. The Bible describes how God *"appeared in the flesh"* (1 Timothy 3:16 NIV).

> **"The Word became flesh and made his dwelling among us. We have seen his glory, the glory of the one and only Son, who came from the Father, full of grace and truth."** *John 1:14 NIV*

- Jesus is referred to as **'Christ'** or **'Messiah'** — the **'Anointed One of God'**.
- Christians see Jesus's time on Earth as God's way of showing how much he **loves** the world. They study the **Gospels** to find out about **Jesus's life**, and to see how they should live their own.

After being baptised by John the Baptist, Jesus began **teaching**. He had many followers, including **12 chosen disciples**.

Some of his key teachings are in the **Sermon on the Mount** (Matthew 5-7) — he taught how the poor and meek are **highly valued** by God, and how **peacemakers** are blessed.

He also taught the importance of **kindness**, such as in the story of the **Good Samaritan** (Luke 10:30-37).

He performed miracles such as **healing** the sick and bringing people **back to life**, showing that he was the **Son of God** and demonstrating God's **love**.

Jesus Christ and Salvation

Salvation is needed before Christians can go to heaven, and **Jesus's actions** made it possible.

Jesus was crucified and resurrected

The Last Supper, Jesus's Arrest and Trial

- Shortly before his death, Jesus and his disciples ate their **Passover** meal in Jerusalem. It was their **final meal** together and became known as the **Last Supper**.

- At the meal, Jesus gave the disciples **bread** saying *"this is my body"* and **wine** saying *"This is my blood"* (Mark 14:22-24 NIV). Luke's Gospel tells us he said *"do this in remembrance of me"* (Luke 22:19 NIV). These words are important to many Christians today who remember Jesus with bread and wine through the **Eucharist** (p.14).

- At the Last Supper, Jesus also **washed** his disciples' **feet**, which teaches Christians about how important it is to **serve** others.

- After the Last Supper, Jesus went to pray in the **Garden of Gethsemane**, where he was **arrested**. The authorities felt **threatened** by Jesus — earlier that week, crowds had called him the '**King of Israel**'.

- He was put on **trial** before the Jewish **high priest** and found guilty of **blasphemy**. Then Jesus was tried before the Roman governor, **Pilate** — he offered to release Jesus, but the crowd said *"Crucify him!"* (Mark 15:13 NIV). He was **flogged**, before being sent to die.

Crucifixion

- Jesus was **crucified** at a place called **Golgotha**, next to two robbers. A sign was fixed to Jesus's cross that read 'The King of the Jews', to record the **charge** against him. Passers-by threw **insults** at Jesus, saying that he could **save others**, but couldn't **save himself**.

- In his suffering, Jesus cried out, *"My God, my God, why have you forsaken me?"* (Mark 15:34 NIV). This shows that Jesus understands how people can feel abandoned in their **suffering**.

- Christians also believe the crucifixion helped to **repair** the **relationship** between God and mankind — the **atonement** (see next page).

Resurrection

- After the crucifixion, Jesus's body was put in a tomb. But he was **resurrected** (brought back to life), and his tomb was found **empty**.

- Jesus talked to two women and told them *"Go and tell my brothers to go to Galilee; there they will see me"* (Matthew 28:10 NIV).

- The resurrection is important to Christians as it shows them that there is **life after death** — **death** becomes **less frightening**.

- It shows them just how **powerful** God is. This power that raised Jesus from the dead gives people the **strength** to live Christian lives.

- Christians also see the resurrection as further **proof** that Jesus is the **Son of God** as he was *"...appointed the Son of God in power by his resurrection from the dead..."* (Romans 1:4 NIV). This strengthens people's **faith**.

> **"...Why do you look for the living among the dead? He is not here; he has risen!"**
> *Luke 24:5-6 NIV*

Roman Catholics refer to the crucifixion, resurrection and ascension of Jesus as 'The Paschal Mystery'.

Jesus going to heaven is called the ascension

- Over the **40 days** after the resurrection, many of Jesus's disciples said they had met him **alive** in various places around **Jerusalem**.

- Then, Jesus '**ascended into Heaven**' to be with God the Father once again. He had **done** what he was sent to **Earth** to do, and it was time for him to **go back** to God.

- In John 14:2, Jesus tells his disciples he will *"prepare a place"* (NIV) for them in heaven. 1 John 2:1 says that, in Jesus, Christians have an 'advocate' with God (someone who will look out for them).

- **Pope Benedict XVI** said that since **Jesus** was **human** and went to be with God, the **ascension** shows there's a **place** for all human beings **with God**.

- The ascension shows **Jesus's power** — he is now *"at the right hand of the mighty God"* (Luke 22:69 NIV).

> **"While he was blessing them, he left them and was taken up into heaven."**
> *Luke 24:51 NIV*

Jesus Christ and Salvation

Jesus died to save humanity

- 'Original sin' (see p.6) means that **everyone** is born capable of sin. Many Christians believe that Jesus's **suffering** and **death** won **forgiveness** for everyone and ensured their **redemption** (freeing them from sin).

- They believe that Jesus was **perfect** (without sin), but God placed **all the sins of the world** on him at his crucifixion. Romans 3:21-26 teaches that his sacrifice **paid** for their sins, so long as they have **faith** in him.

- Jesus's actions brought about the **reconciliation** between God and humanity — known as the **atonement**.

- His power and goodness were so **great** that after he was crucified, death couldn't keep hold of him.

- However, **not** all Christians believe that Jesus **had to die** to pay for people's sins:

> "For God so loved the world that he gave his one and only Son, that whoever believes in him shall not perish but have eternal life. For God did not send his Son into the world to condemn the world, but to save the world through him."
> *John 3:16-17 NIV*

1 Corinthians 13:5 says that love *"keeps no record of wrongs"* (NIV). Many Christians think that Jesus's death **wasn't required** for a loving and merciful God to be able to **forgive** people's sins.

Some people argue that it was Jesus's **ministry** that showed people how to be free from sin — he showed them how to live their lives in a **Godly** way.

Some say Jesus's death shows **God's love** for humankind through his **willingness** to **suffer** and die as humans do. His resurrection showed how God could **triumph** over **sin** and **death**, so people don't have to fear **evil**.

Christians must seek salvation to get to heaven

- To achieve salvation, Christians believe they must have faith in Jesus.

> "Salvation is found in no one else..." *Acts 4:12 NIV*

- Salvation is only possible through God's grace — God showing favour to those who haven't earned it.

> "For it is by grace you have been saved, through faith... it is the gift of God" *Ephesians 2:8 NIV*

salvation
the soul being saved from death and sin, allowing it to reach heaven

BUT...

People can't just **say** they believe — if they're a true believer they'll try to **live** a Christian life. The Bible contains many **laws**, such as the **Ten Commandments**, which provide Christians with **guidance** on how they should behave. Everyone will **sin**, but the laws mean they'll *"become conscious of ... sin"* (Romans 3:20 NIV) and *"turn to God in repentance"* (Acts 20:21 NIV).

- The Holy Spirit helps Christians to follow the teachings of God and his laws and keep their faith, helping them to find salvation.

Revision can save you from exam failure...

'Jesus's death had to happen in order to save humanity.' Evaluate this statement.
Include arguments for and against, examples from Christian teachings, and a conclusion. [12]

Different Forms of Worship

Worship is a Christian's way of expressing their **love** of, **respect** for, and **devotion** to God.

Christian denominations have *different forms* of worship

- For Christians, Sunday is the '**Lord's Day**', when they celebrate the **Sabbath**. Most churches have their main service on a **Sunday morning**.
- Worship often includes prayers, readings from the Bible, a sermon and the Eucharist (see p.14) — the different denominations place varying amounts of **importance** on each, creating **differences** in worship.

> **Sabbath**
> *the holy day of rest*

> If you're studying Catholic Christianity, just read the relevant column of the table below.

Some worship is *liturgical*

- '**Liturgical**' means that services follow a **set pattern** written out by the Church.

	Anglican Worship	Catholic Worship	Orthodox Worship
OVERVIEW	• Sunday morning services **usually** include the Eucharist. • Worship is guided by the '**Common Worship**' book, based on the Book of Common Prayer from 1662.	• Sunday morning services **always** include the Eucharist. • Catholics call the Eucharist '**Mass**'. • The '**Roman Missal**' sets out the contents of the service.	• The main Sunday service is the '**Divine Liturgy**', which centres on the Eucharist. • The service is usually based on the liturgy of **St John Chrysostom**.
THE SERVICE	• A **confession** of sin and a request for God's mercy is said by everyone. *This is called the '**penitential rite**' by Catholics.* • There are readings (including one **gospel** reading) and a sermon — this part is known as the '**liturgy of the Word**'. The **Nicene** or **Apostle's Creed** is then recited. • The priest says prayers over bread and wine — this is called the '**liturgy of the Eucharist**'. • Then the congregation says the **Lord's Prayer** (see p.16) and 'shares the peace' by shaking hands. They receive the bread and wine. *Catholics call this the '**rite of Communion**'.*		• Services contain **similar** elements to Anglican and Catholic ones — a sermon, Bible readings, the Nicene Creed and blessing of bread and wine. • They include the '**Litany**', where the priest says **prayers** and the congregation responds with 'Lord have mercy'. Worshippers **sing** or **chant** for most of the service. • Services are often **longer** than most Anglican and Catholic services, and people **stand** for the majority of the time.

- For many, public worship helps them to feel involved in a **wider Christian community**.
- It can also help them feel **closer** to Jesus, as they believe he is there in the church with them.
- Following **traditions** also helps Christians to feel **connected** to other worshippers throughout **history**.

> "For where two or three gather in my name, there am I with them."
> *Matthew 18:20 NIV*

Different Forms of Worship

Other worship is non-liturgical

- The worship of the **Society of Friends** (Quakers) is non-liturgical, and it is usually **unstructured**.
- Worshippers sit together in **silence**, but they are free to pray or speak **out loud**.

- **Methodist** services **don't** have to follow a set structure, but there is a 'Methodist Worship Book' with suggested liturgy for parts of worship, e.g. the **Eucharist**.
- Services feature **hymns**, **readings**, a **sermon** and **prayers**. The **Eucharist** also takes place, but **not every week**.

- Worship in **Evangelical** Churches (e.g. **Pentecostals**) is often **spontaneous**. Worshippers believe they're inspired by the **Spirit** — this is called '**charismatic** worship'.
- It might inspire them to pray, clap, dance or shout. Sometimes they '**speak in tongues**' — praying in an unrecognisable language.

Some Christians prefer the **freedom** of worshipping God in a **less structured** way. Others view non-liturgical worship as **unsuitable** for the level of **respect** that religious services require.

Some Christians also engage in private worship

- Many Christians worship informally **at home** (not just on Sundays). This can be anything from saying **grace** before a meal to singing **worship songs** with family, to reading the **Bible** or praying (see p.16).
- Lots of Christians worship **both** publicly and privately — private worship can help them keep God in mind throughout their **everyday lives**. Some also find greater **freedom** in private worship — they decide how they worship God and so feel a **better connection** with God.

EXAM QUESTION

Who's singing out of tune? Hymn...

Give two reasons why some Christians might prefer liturgical worship.　　　　　　*[2]*

The Sacraments

Sacraments play a key role in **worship** and **belief** for many Christians.

Different denominations believe in different sacraments

- Roman Catholic and Orthodox Churches believe in **seven sacraments** (see p.15), but most Protestants accept only **baptism** and the **Eucharist** as sacraments — they believe only these two were **prescribed** by Jesus in the **Gospels**. Many believe that the sacraments bring people **closer to God**.

- Quakers and the Salvation Army don't celebrate the Eucharist or any other sacraments, seeing them as **unnecessary symbols** for the inward acceptance of God's grace.

> **sacrament**
> *a ceremony (usually carried out by a minister or priest) through which Christians believe they receive God's grace — it is a sign of God's grace working within them*

Baptism is an important sacrament for many Christians

- Baptism is seen as a sacrament because Jesus was baptised. After his resurrection, he told his disciples to go out and baptise people.

- Baptism makes someone a member of God's family and welcomes them to the Church. Some Christians believe that baptising cleanses people from the original sin that everyone is born with.

- Babies are baptised in many denominations, e.g. Anglican, Catholic and Methodist. (They will also baptise adults if they weren't baptised as children and want to join the Church.)

> **"...go and make disciples of all nations, baptising them in the name of the Father and of the Son and of the Holy Spirit"** *Matthew 28:19 NIV*

> **"no one can enter the kingdom of God unless they are born of water and the Spirit"** *John 3:5 NIV*

A sign of the cross is made on the baby, and in many Churches holy water is poured three times over the forehead (in the name of the Father, Son and Holy Spirit). Orthodox Christians baptise babies by total immersion.

Denominations that baptise babies also usually have confirmation — a person 'confirms' their faith when they reach an age that they can declare it themselves.

But some denominations — for example Baptists and Pentecostals — believe you shouldn't be baptised until you're old enough to accept Christianity for yourself. They hold believers' baptisms, when adults who wish to join the Church are baptised by total immersion.

There are many different understandings of the Eucharist

The **Eucharist** is where Christians remember the **Last Supper** (see p.10) with **bread and wine**. Many denominations see it as a **sacrament**, but have **different beliefs** about the bread and wine, and transubstantiation:

> **transubstantiation**
> *the idea that the bread and wine used become the flesh and blood of Christ*

Catholics believe in **transubstantiation** and every Mass is a re-enactment of Christ's sacrifice (see p.10). They believe that they receive the saving power of Jesus into themselves through the bread and wine.

Lutherans, **Methodists** and most **Anglicans** believe Holy Communion is more than just an 'intellectual' commemoration of the Last Supper — it's a re-enactment. They believe that there is a 'real presence' of Christ in the bread and wine, but they don't believe that transubstantiation occurs.

> **"Transubstantiation... in the Supper of the Lord, cannot be proved by holy Writ..."** *39 Articles XXVIII*

Baptists view the bread and wine as **symbols**, but believe that God is **present** through the act of Christians **coming together** to share Communion. The **bread** and **non-alcoholic wine** are set out on a simple **table**. The **bread** is later **offered** from person to person, and the **wine** drunk from small **individual** cups.

Denominations which place **more meaning** on the bread and wine (e.g. Catholicism and Orthodox) hold Eucharists **more often** — they believe it's essential for sustaining their **relationship** with God. They tend to use a more ornate table (an **altar**), and have more **ritual** surrounding the Eucharist (e.g. using **incense**). **Catholics** will be given bread by the priest and drink wine from a **shared cup**. **Orthodox** Christians are given the bread and wine **together** on a special **spoon**.

REVISION TASK

Immerse yourself and learn all about baptism...

Close the book and jot down the different denominations' beliefs about baptism and the Eucharist.

The Sacraments

Catholics believe there are **seven** specific sacraments through which God can communicate his **grace** directly. Some see the **whole world** as **sacramental** — they can experience **God's grace** through his creation.

The seven sacraments — God shows his grace

> "The seven sacraments touch all the stages and all the important moments of Christian life..." *Catechism of the Catholic Church, 1210*

(1) BAPTISM

This marks a person's official **entry** into the Church (see p.14).

(2) CONFIRMATION

In this ceremony, a Christian (often a teenager) **renews** the vows made on their behalf at baptism. **Confirmation** is believed to **strengthen the ties** of the confirmed to the Church and to God. In Catholic confirmations, the bishop anoints the believer's forehead with holy oil called **chrism**.

(3) RECONCILIATION

This involves **confession** of a sin, following by **contrition**, **penance** and **absolution**. This is how Catholics seek to obtain **forgiveness** for the sins they commit. They must **tell** a priest about any **sinful** things that they've done. The priest will give a **penance** (a certain number of prayers to be said, or an action to be done) and will then pronounce **absolution** (God's forgiveness).

(4) ANOINTING THE SICK

A priest or bishop anoints a **seriously unwell person** with the **oil of the sick**. Catholics believe that, through this, the **Holy Spirit** renews the person's **faith** and **strength** to **cope** with their illness and **accept** their suffering. The anointing is also believed to **link** the person's suffering to **Christ's** suffering, allow their **sins** to be forgiven and to **heal** them, if that is **God's will**.

(5) MATRIMONY

Catholics believe Jesus performed his **first miracle** at a **wedding**. They believe that God is **present** at the ceremony and **promises** are made before him — couples joined in **Holy Matrimony** should be together for **life**. As it's a sacrament, the union is a way that God **blesses** the couple, and he also blesses them **through** one another.

(6) HOLY ORDERS

This is the process by which men are ordained as **deacons**, **priests** or **bishops**. Like matrimony, it is a **commitment** that they make for life.

(7) EUCHARIST

The Eucharist (Mass) is seen as *"the source and summit of the Christian life"* (Catechism of the Catholic Church 1324). Receiving the **body** and **blood** of Christ (see p.14) **joins** people together in their faith and gives them the **strength** to live Christian lives and face any **problems** they may encounter.

> "...in the breaking of the Eucharistic bread, we are taken up into communion with Him and with one another." *Lumen gentium Chapter 1 Paragraph 7:53*

Some of the bread and wine that is **blessed** but **not consumed** is kept in the church — people believe **Jesus** is still **present** in it, and **focus** on it as they pray and express their love for Jesus. This is known as 'eucharistic adoration'.

Catholic funerals have three parts

The funeral rite isn't a sacrament, but it's important.

- The **Vigil of Prayer** takes place the day before the funeral and is sometimes held at home. Readings and prayers form the service, which aims to **help** family and friends prepare to say **goodbye**.

- Attending a funeral allows Catholics to join together in **praying** to God to **take care** of the person.

The **Funeral Liturgy** often includes Holy Communion (the '**Requiem Mass**'). Its purpose is to pray for the soul of the dead person.	The coffin is covered with a white cloth (a **pall**) as it is carried into the church.	The coffin is sprinkled with **holy water** and the priest says, "In the waters of baptism [name] died with Christ, and rose with him to new life. May s/he now share with him in eternal glory."	The coffin is later sprinkled again and perfumed with **incense**. The **Paschal candle** sits beside it.

- The **Committal** is a short ceremony that happens at the **cemetery** (or the **crematorium** if the person wished to be cremated). The priest says "ashes to ashes, dust to dust" as the body goes back to the **earth**.

REVISION TASK

Big Cats Rarely Ask Me 'Ham or Egg?'...

...is a good way to remember the first letters of the sacraments. Try summarising each sacrament in one or two sentences <u>in your own words</u> — make sure you know why each one is important.

Christianity & Catholic Christianity

Prayer and Pilgrimage

Prayer and pilgrimage are both ways in which Christians might **strengthen** their **relationship** with God.

Prayer puts people in touch with their God

- **Prayer** is when believers mentally or vocally **communicate** with God — it should be part of **daily life**.

- Prayer can come in many **different forms**:

> "Prayer is the raising of one's mind and heart to God"
> *Catechism of the Catholic Church 2559*

Thanksgiving — thanking God

Supplication — asking God for something

Adoration — worshipping God

Confession — admitting your sins

Intercession — asking God to help other people

- Believers draw **comfort** from the fact that God is listening to them. They also listen for what **he** is saying to **them** — many believe prayer helps them to **find out** what God wants them to do in **life**.

Formal prayer

- Most denominations have **formal**, **set prayers** that are Church tradition — they can be said during acts of worship in church, and also in private.

- The **Lord's Prayer** is very important. It's based on the words **Jesus** used when he told his disciples **how** to **pray**. It covers key **themes** — e.g. the idea that God is '**Our Father**' and he **provides** for people's physical needs.

> "This, then, is how you should pray: 'Our Father in heaven, hallowed be your name, your kingdom come, your will be done, on earth as it is in heaven. Give us today our daily bread. And forgive us our debts, as we also have forgiven our debtors. And lead us not into temptation, but deliver us from the evil one.' " *Matthew 6:9-13 NIV*

Informal prayer

- **Informal prayers** are where the individual talks to God in their **own words**. They're sometimes called '**extempore**' prayers, and can be used in worship and privately.

- Informal prayers are more **personal** and show the individual's **connection** with God — many Christians **prefer** them to set prayers.

Catholics have different forms of popular piety

You only need to read this bit if you're studying Catholic Christianity.

- Catholics use the **Rosary** when praying. The **cross** is **held** when reciting the Apostles' Creed, and prayers are said as the **beads** are **moved** through the fingers, e.g. Ave Maria (Hail Mary). The beads represent the **key events** in Christianity (known as **mysteries**), such as the birth, death and resurrection of Jesus — the rosary helps people **think** about these while praying.

- The '**Stations of the Cross**' are pictures in church of Jesus's **suffering** — Catholics use them as a **focus** for **contemplation** on these events.

- Some **disagree** with these forms of 'popular piety'. Some Protestants think the rosary encourages prayers to be repeated **without** giving **thought** to the words themselves.

- Many Protestants wouldn't say the **Hail Mary** prayer, as most **don't** believe in praying to **Mary**.

- Some people might argue that praying while focusing on the Stations of the Cross creates a **danger** of **worshipping idols**.

Beliefs, Teachings and Practices — Christianity & Catholic Christianity

Prayer and Pilgrimage

Pilgrimages *can help believers feel* nearer *to God*

- Pilgrimages aren't **compulsory** in Christianity, but many see them as **important**. Luke 2:41-43 tells the story of the pilgrimage **Jesus** and his **parents** made to **Jerusalem**.

> **"Pilgrimages evoke our earthly journey toward heaven..."**
> *Catechism of the Catholic Church 2691*

- Christians make pilgrimages for a variety of **reasons**:

| to seek healing | to seek forgiveness | to connect to God | to deepen their faith | to escape normal life | to concentrate more on religion |

- Pilgrims can also **learn** from each other. The journey **reflects** the path they're trying to follow towards God.

There are various places *Christians might visit*

- People may visit places that are **significant** in Christianity. For example:

Jerusalem $\Rightarrow$ Christians can visit key places in **Jesus's life** and **death** here.

Rome $\Rightarrow$ Roman Catholics often visit **Rome** because it is the home of the **Pope**.

- Some Christians, especially **Catholics**, make pilgrimages to **shrines** where Mary has appeared.
- These include **Walsingham** (popular with some Anglicans as well as Catholics) and **Lourdes**.
- Catholics also visit shrines to **saints**.

LOURDES

- The **water** in Lourdes is said to have **healing** properties which can **cure** ill health.
- Lots of people believe **miracles** take place there.
- Some Christians see shrines such as Lourdes as being too **commercialised**, with **too many people**.

Protestants are more likely to visit places they can find **peace** to study the Bible and pray. For example:
- the quiet island of **Iona** (which has a long history of Christianity)
- **Taizé**, where they can join worship at the monastery.

- Some Christians regard pilgrimage as **unnecessary** — they believe that the journey inside is what matters.

EXAM TIP

I make a daily pilgrimage to the biscuit tin...

Make sure you know why people go on pilgrimages and the differences between the famous Christian pilgrimage sites, e.g. some are famous for visions, others for events that happened there.

| Christianity | # Christmas and Easter |

Christmas and Easter are the two most important **celebrations** in the Christian calendar.

Christmas is a celebration of Jesus's birth

Christmas celebrates how Jesus was born in **Bethlehem** — there he was worshipped by **shepherds** after an **angel** told them that *"a Saviour has been born to you; he is the Messiah, the Lord"* (Luke 2:11 NIV).

 Christmas is celebrated by most Christians on **25th December**, but for **Orthodox** Christians it's **7th January**.

- Christmas comes after a period called **Advent**, which begins four Sundays before Christmas.
- Advent is significant for many Christians as it's time they spend **getting ready** to celebrate **Jesus's birth** — a time for **prayer** and **reflection**.
- **Advent candles** are lit in homes and churches, and children may use **Advent calendars** to count off the days until Christmas.

- Lots of Roman Catholic, Orthodox and Anglican churches have a '**Midnight Mass**' to welcome Christmas Day, and most Christians go to church on **Christmas morning** to **celebrate**.
- Many churches hold services in the days **after Christmas**, carrying on to **Epiphany** (6th January) — the day that the **Magi** (wise men) went to see Jesus in Bethlehem.

Customs **vary** around the world. **Gifts** are exchanged to symbolise the fact that Jesus was **God's gift** to the world, and to remember how the Magi *"presented him with gifts of gold, frankincense and myrrh"* (Matthew 2:11 NIV).

- Some Christians dislike modern Christmas **traditions** and **customs**, e.g. **Santa Claus** (Father Christmas), giving **expensive presents**, and **excessive eating** and **drinking**.
- They believe that some of these modern traditions **devalue** the **true meaning** of Christmas. Others feel that it has retained too much **pagan** influence, such as Christmas trees.

Christmas and Easter

Easter celebrates Jesus's resurrection

- Easter is the most **important** festival for Christians, since it celebrates **Jesus's victory** over death, when God raised him **back to life** after his crucifixion (see p.10).

- This reminds people that God **loves** them so much that he was **willing** to suffer death on the cross, and this gives them hope of **eternal life**.

> **"And if Christ has not been raised, our preaching is useless and so is your faith"**
> *1 Corinthians 15:14*

This outlines how important the Resurrection is for Christians and their beliefs.

LENT
- **Lent** is the **40 days** before Easter.
- On **Ash Wednesday** (the first day of Lent), ash is put on believers' **foreheads** to show they're sorry for their **sins**.
- Some Christians **fast** (**eat less** and have only **simple food**) during Lent to mark when Jesus fasted for 40 days in the desert. They **stop fasting** on **Easter Sunday**.

- The lead-up to **Easter Day**, the day of resurrection, is marked by a number of important events:

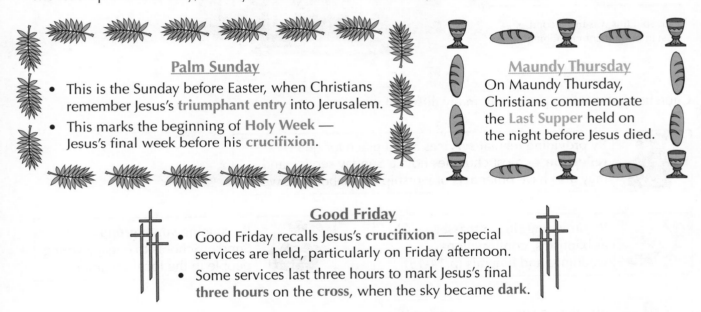

Palm Sunday
- This is the Sunday before Easter, when Christians remember Jesus's **triumphant entry** into Jerusalem.
- This marks the beginning of **Holy Week** — Jesus's final week before his **crucifixion**.

Maundy Thursday
On Maundy Thursday, Christians commemorate the **Last Supper** held on the night before Jesus died.

Good Friday
- Good Friday recalls Jesus's **crucifixion** — special services are held, particularly on Friday afternoon.
- Some services last three hours to mark Jesus's final **three hours** on the **cross**, when the sky became **dark**.

- **Easter Day** is a **joyous** occasion, when Jesus's resurrection is celebrated:

- Some churches hold services on the Saturday night, and most have **special services** on the Sunday morning.
- The **Paschal candle** is lit during services in Anglican and Catholic churches. Worshippers light their own candle from its flame, which represents Jesus as the **Light of the World**.
- Some churches hold **sunrise services** to remember how Mary Magdalene discovered at daybreak that Jesus's tomb was empty. The rising of the **sun** is symbolic of **God's Son** rising from the dead.
- **Eggs** are associated with Easter as a symbol of **new life**.
  - However, some view chocolate Easter eggs as **commercialisation** of the festival.

REVISION TASK

Learning about Easter is an eggcellent way to gain marks...

Working from Lent to Easter Sunday, draw a timeline of Christian Easter celebrations.
Next to each day, scribble down what happens and then check your answers against this page.

The Work of the Church

Churches aren't just about holding services. They're active in the **local community** too.

Churches play an *important role* in the *local community*

Most communities in the UK have access to at least one church. The role of the **local church** is to put the **Christian faith into action** — this includes **caring** for the community, as seen in lots of Christian teaching:

"...be shepherds of God's flock that is under your care, watching over them... being examples to the flock" 1 Peter 5:2-3

This is what is expected of the leaders of the church when asked to set an example for the congregation through their actions.

"Every social group must take account of the needs and legitimate aspirations of other groups, and even of the general welfare of the entire human family." Gaudium et spes (paragraph 26)

This is a key Catholic document of the Second Vatican Council

"Love your neighbour as yourself" Mark 12:31

Jesus said this was the second most important commandment.

Churches put this into practice in many **different ways**:

 By providing regular **services** and a place for **quiet reflection** — most churches hold a Sunday service and may also have other acts of worship throughout the week.

 By providing **rites of passage** such as baptisms, confirmations, weddings and funerals (p.14-15).

 By running **youth groups** and Sunday Schools to engage young people in the local community.

 By offering **support** and **advice** to people in need — e.g. visiting and praying for people in hospital.

 Some churchgoers work as **Street Pastors** — they volunteer in towns and cities on **Friday** and **Saturday nights** to support anyone in need of help. This demonstrates Christian love.

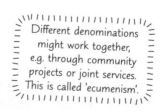 Different denominations might work together, e.g. through community projects or joint services. This is called 'ecumenism'.

 Some **foodbanks** in the UK are run by churches. People **donate** food which the foodbank then **distributes** to those who need it the most.

 Many churches also raise money for **charity**.

 EXAM QUESTION

It's my mission to get you to learn this page...

Give two examples of the work that churches do in their local communities. [2]

The Work of the Church

Evangelism tells people about Christianity

- In Mark 16:15, Jesus told his disciples to *"Go into all the world and preach the gospel to all creation"* (NIV). Many Christians believe that they should be prepared to do the same.

> **evangelism**
> *spreading the Christian message with the aim of converting people*

> **"As the Father has sent me, I am sending you."** *John 20:21 NIV*

- They believe that by evangelising they can help people **discover** their **real purpose** in life and find **salvation**. They feel **excited** to tell other people about **Jesus's love**.

> Pope Francis said *"The primary reason for evangelizing is the love of Jesus which we have received..."* (Evangelii Gaudium 264).

- For some, evangelism is about telling people **directly** about God. This can sometimes cause problems — people may feel **offended**. Others try to **demonstrate** God's love through their actions, to bring people **closer** to God.

- Here are a few different types of evangelism:

Gideons distribute copies of the **Bible** in places like hotels and care homes.	Churches might ask the congregation to **bring** along a **friend** who wouldn't normally go to church.	The **Salvation Army** helps people by providing **hot meals** and **beds** for homeless people. They also attend **emergencies**, such as floods.

- As church attendance falls, evangelism is increasingly important. The Church of England and Church in Wales are finding ways to interest **new people** in churches that **don't** follow the **traditional model** — for example worshipping in alternative venues like **cafés**, or creating a café **atmosphere** in church. Through initiatives called '**Fresh Expressions**' and '**Pioneer Ministry**', they offer a new approach for modern society.

- **Missionaries** spread the Christian message **abroad**. Many aren't there to preach, but to use their **skills** to help **disadvantaged people** — e.g. a doctor might choose to work in a poor country. These people demonstrate the message of Christianity through their **actions**.

Reconciliation works towards peace and unity

- Christians believe in justice — all people are equal in God's eyes, so they should be treated fairly. Christian organisations help people being treated unfairly due to war, religious persecution or poverty.

- In Matthew 5:9 Jesus said *"Blessed are the peacemakers"* (NIV). Christians believe that reconciliation (coming together and making peace) is needed between people who have been in conflict with one another — just as Jesus brought God and humankind together through the atonement (p.11).

- These are two examples of organisations that work for reconciliation:

The Corrymeela Community

- The **Corrymeela Community** in Northern Ireland was founded to help **heal** the country's political and religious **divisions**.
- It works with people in areas where there is **tension** and strives to help people **understand** each other and **reconcile** through group activities and discussions.

Pax Christi

- **Pax Christi** is an international **Catholic** organisation working for **human rights**, **disarmament** and **peace**.
- They believe **violence** should be **avoided**, and they work to create a world where people can live in **harmony**.

Christianity & Catholic Christianity	# The Work of the Church

Organisations and churches help persecuted Christians

- Millions around the world **suffer** for being Christians — some endure **prison sentences** or even **death**.
- Organisations give support by providing **Bibles** so people can continue worshipping in secret. They offer **training** to church members and **support** people who have lost their homes.
- Churches **pray** for the persecuted and may send **money**. Christians might **petition** for **government** help.

Christian charities help those in need

- In the story of the **sheep** and **goats** (Matthew 25:31-46), Jesus explains that people who have been **good** (the sheep) and have helped others will be **looked after** by God. People who **haven't** (the goats) will **suffer**. The story tells Christians that they are **helping Jesus** when they help others.
- Because of this, **charity** is very important to many Christians. But it's **not** all about giving **money** — it must be done with **love**. In 1 Corinthians 13:3, St Paul said *"If I give all I possess to the poor... but do not have love, I gain nothing"* (NIV).

Christian Aid works **globally** to relieve poverty. They set up projects in the developing world, drawing on the skills of **local people**. The organisation also aims to change **government policy** to help reduce the suffering of the world's poor, e.g. through **debt relief**, and **fair-trade** products.

CAFOD (Catholic Agency for Overseas Development) works to fight **poverty** and **injustice** around the world. They work through churches, helping in **emergencies**, but also giving people the **skills** to help themselves.

Tearfund is an **evangelical** organisation — it helps communities with projects run **through** their **churches**. Their work includes trying to end **hunger**, resolving **tension** in conflict zones and helping **refugees**. They also help areas hit by **natural disasters**.

Christian Aid and CAFOD believe in **development** — 'helping people to help themselves', **whatever** their faith.

There are many Catholic charities

> ⟵ This section is only for people studying Catholic Christianity.

Evangelii Gaudium (187) says that Catholics should strive to **help** the **poor** *"to be fully a part of society"*. **CAFOD** (see above) is a Roman Catholic organisation, and there are many others that help those in need:

Trócaire ⟹ Trócaire, part of the Irish Catholic Church, **provides aid** abroad. They help people **escape poverty**, but also help in **emergencies**.

SVP ⟹ The **St Vincent de Paul Society** (SVP) helps people in **poverty**. They provide support by **visiting** the isolated and ill, helping them with **daily tasks**, providing **schemes** and **clubs** to help the disabled, and **donating food** to the homeless.

Missio ⟹ **Missio** is an organisation that **supports churches** abroad that are **struggling** to fund themselves, e.g. by **training** church leaders. It also runs projects to provide **education** and **healthcare** for children living in poverty.

Sheep — good, goats — baaaad...

EXAM TIP

In the exam, some of the 4 mark questions will ask you how a particular belief influences the people of a religion. You'll have to describe two ways in detail in order to get full marks.

Beliefs, Teachings and Practices — Christianity & Catholic Christianity

Revision Summary

That was a lot to take in there, so now see how you get on with these exam-style questions. Answer 1-12 if you're studying Christianity. If you're studying Catholic Christianity, answer them all except 4 and 5. If there's anything you can't answer, go back through the section and have another go when you've re-read it.

Christianity and Catholic Christianity

Let's get cracking — have a go at these 1 mark multiple choice questions.

1) Which of the following words means that God is all-powerful?
   a) just   b) omnipotent   c) immanent   d) benevolent

2) Which of the following is Jesus's return to heaven to be with God the Father?
   a) resurrection   b) Last Supper   c) ascension   d) crucifixion

You've found your feet now, so let's jump up to 2 marks. Make two brief points to scoop both the marks.

3) Give two beliefs about the Last Judgement.

4) Give two examples of different types of evil. ⇐ *Only answer these questions if you're studying Christianity.*

5) Give two ways that Christians celebrate Easter. ⇐

For the 4 mark questions, you need to give two points and develop them to get full marks.

6) Explain two contrasting Christian views about the creation story.

7) Explain two ways in which belief in salvation influences Christians today.   *Organise your points and write concisely in the 4 and 5 mark questions — make your points clearly.*

8) Explain two contrasting Christian views on the Eucharist.

All the way up to 5 marks now. Explain your points and make sure you refer to a sacred text.

9) Explain two Christian teachings about the Trinity.

10) Explain two beliefs that Christians hold about Jesus's resurrection.   *Turn to the 'Do Well in Your Exam' section for tips on writing essays.*

11) Explain two reasons why evangelism is important to Christians.

Now it's the one you've been looking forward to — the 12 mark question.
You'll get a list of things that you've got to have in your answer, which is handy for creating a plan.
You'll be asked to give arguments for and against a statement, so be sure to include plenty of detail.

12) 'Pilgrimage is the best way for a Christian to develop their relationship with God.'
    Evaluate this statement. Your answer should include the following:
    • examples from Christian teachings   • arguments that disagree with the statement
    • arguments that support the statement   • a conclusion

Catholic Christianity

13) Which of the following is not part of the Catholic funeral rite? [1]
    a) Reconciliation   b) Committal   c) Requiem Mass   d) Vigil of Prayer

14) Give two beliefs that Catholics hold about purgatory. [2]

15) Explain two contrasting Christian views about the Rosary. [4]

16) Explain two reasons why Catholics believe it's important to 'love your neighbour'.
    You should refer to religious teaching or sacred texts. [5]   *There are an extra 3 marks for SPaG for this question, so check your writing carefully.*

17) 'The sacraments are the most important part of a Catholic's faith.' ⇐
    Evaluate this statement. Your answer should include the following:
    • examples from Catholic teachings   • arguments that disagree with the statement
    • arguments that support the statement   • a conclusion. [12]

Buddhism	# Introduction to Buddhism

Buddhism is a popular religion in **Asia**, but in **Great Britain** there are only a **small number** of Buddhists.

Buddhism is a very old religion

- Buddhism is based on the teachings of a man called **Siddhartha Gautama**. He was a rich prince from **Nepal**, born over **2 400 years ago**, who later became known as **the Buddha** (see p.28).
- Buddhists follow the Buddha's **teachings** in order to avoid **suffering** and find out the **truth** about life — this is called **enlightenment**.

There are many different branches of Buddhism

There's more about the different branches on page 27.

Each branch of Buddhism has its own **traditions** and **practices**:

Theravada	Mahayana	
• Theravada Buddhism is popular in **Sri Lanka** and **South East Asia**. • Many Theravada Buddhists live a monastic life. This means that they live in a community of monks and spend a lot of time meditating.	• Mahayana Buddhism is popular in **Korea**, **Japan**, **Tibet**, **Taiwan** and **China**. • Mahayana Buddhists think that anybody can overcome **suffering** and find **peace** by living a **good** and **selfless life** (not just monks). **Helping others** is very important.	
	Zen	**Pure Land**
	• Zen is a part of the **Mahayana branch**. • Zen Buddhists use **meditation** to try to understand the **truth** about life.	• Pure Land is a part of the **Mahayana branch**. • Pure Land Buddhists believe they will be **reborn** into a **paradise world** called **Pure Land**. A large part of their practice involves **chanting**.

There are lots of sacred texts in Buddhism

When the Buddha was alive, **writing** wasn't very common, so he didn't **write down** any of his teachings. Instead, people passed on his teachings by **telling others** about them. **Hundreds of years** after the Buddha died, people did start to **write all this down**.

The **Pali Canon** is the collection of sacred texts used by **Theravada Buddhists**. It is also known as the **Tipitaka** (meaning **three baskets**) because it is split into **three main parts**:

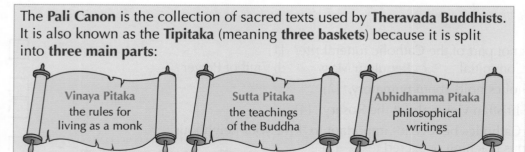

Vinaya Pitaka
the rules for
living as a monk

Sutta Pitaka
the teachings
of the Buddha

Abhidhamma Pitaka
philosophical
writings

The Mahayana Buddhists' sacred texts are made up of a collection of over two thousand sutras (teachings), which reflect their beliefs. They also accept the Pali Canon as a sacred text.

Buddhism has lots of different words for the same thing...

Because Buddhism is so old, some words have several spellings and there's often more than one word for the same thing. Don't worry too much about this — just make sure you can spell one version correctly.

The Dhamma and Dependent Arising

The word **Dhamma** (meaning "**law**" or "**teaching**") refers to the things the **Buddha taught**. An important part of his teaching is the concept of **dependent arising** — everything is **dependent** on something else.

The Dhamma is the Buddha's teachings

- The Dhamma is all the **teachings** that the Buddha gave while he was alive.
- This includes **stories** he told and **sermons** (lectures) he gave to groups of people.
- The most famous part of the Dhamma is the **Four Noble Truths** (see p.29-30).

The Dhamma is one of the Three Jewels of Buddhism

The **Three Jewels of Buddhism** are the three things that Buddhists use to **guide them**. Buddhists get **guidance** from:

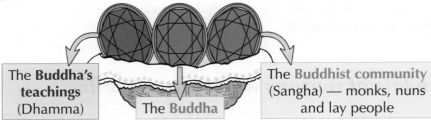

The **Buddha's teachings** (Dhamma)

The **Buddha**

The **Buddhist community** (Sangha) — monks, nuns and lay people

Buddhists believe everything is dependent on something else

- Buddhists believe that **everything exists** because **something else exists**, e.g. a person exists because of their parents, and their parents exist because of their parents, and so on. Everything is **caused by something else** and that, in turn, **affects other things**.
- Buddhists also believe that things in our **previous lives** have an effect on our **current life** and things in our current life will have an effect on **the future**.
- These causes and effects are called the **links of dependent arising**:

> **Dependent Arising (Paticcasamupada)** the idea that everything is connected and all existence is caused by something else

Past causes from a previous life	Present causes from your current life	Present effects	Future effects
The way you behaved in a **previous life** can affect the type of life you are **reborn** into, e.g. being **greedy** could mean you are born into an **unhappy** life (see p.33).	Your **personality** may be the result of the way you behaved in a **previous life**, e.g. **greediness** in your previous life might mean you are now the kind of person that can **never be satisfied**.	**Craving** things in this life (like food or possessions) means that you will develop and **attachment** to these things.	**Cravings** and **attachments** can affect you in the **future**, e.g. being **greedy** with money might lead you to become **jealous** of others with money.

- The Buddha believed that we should try to **understand** dependent arising so that we can **break free** from these causes and effects.
  - E.g. if you enjoy chocolate cake, you should just have chocolate cake **every now and again** rather than eating **too much** of it. This is because of the **negative effects** that **craving** things has on the future.

Doing well in your exams is dependent on you revising...

Get into the habit of practising by having a go at this exam-style question.
Explain two ways in which Buddhists believe that dependent arising affects their lives. [4]

| Buddhism | **The Three Marks of Existence** |

This page is all about **human existence** and **suffering** — it sounds pretty heavy, but it's **important stuff**.

There are *three Marks of Existence*

The Buddha taught that all of existence has **three things in common**, known as the **Three Marks of Existence** or the three **lakshanas** (characteristics):

1

Anicca (impermanence)
Everything is constantly **changing** and will eventually **die**, e.g. humans beings are always **getting older**. Buddhists believe this is true of **all things**, not just humans — e.g. **relationships** won't last forever, and **buildings** won't last forever.

2

Anatta (no fixed self)
Everything is made up of hundreds of **different parts** (mental and physical). For humans, there is **no individual part** that makes you who you are. Buddhists do not believe that humans have a **soul**.

3

Dukkha (suffering)
Everything **suffers**. Humans can suffer and feel **unsatisfied** with their life. Suffering can be experienced **mentally** (e.g. feeling sad) or **physically** (e.g. breaking a bone).

There are lots of *reasons* why *humans suffer*

There's more about suffering on pages 29-30.

	Humans suffer because...	
	...of **mental** and **physical pain**. This can be caused by lots of **different factors**, e.g. not getting the grade you wanted in an exam. This is called **dukkha-dukkha**.	**"... separation from the liked is suffering; not getting what you wish for is suffering."** *Samyutta Nikaya 56.11*
	...everything is **impermanent** (anicca). Nothing can last forever and this causes both **mental suffering** (e.g. an old person might feel sad that they are no longer young) and **physical suffering** (e.g. arthritis from old age). This is called **viparinama-dukkha**.	**"Rebirth is suffering; old age is suffering; illness is suffering; death is suffering"** *Samyutta Nikaya 56.11*
	...of a **general dissatisfaction with life**. This is often because humans are attached to things they cannot hold on to (such as relationships, jobs or objects) and this causes **suffering**. This is called **sankhara-dukkha**.	

Humans should *learn about* the Three Marks of Existence

- Buddhists believe that humans should **teach themselves** about the Three Marks of Existence so they can **suffer less**.
- Buddhists think that people are constantly **attaching themselves** to **physical things** (e.g. money) and **emotional things** (e.g. people) — this leads to **suffering** because these things are **impermanent** and cannot last forever.
- Becoming **aware** of the Three Marks of Existence will lead to **less suffering**. E.g. if you are aware that relationships with people will not last forever and you can **accept** this fact, then you will **suffer less** when somebody you know dies.

EXAM QUESTION

You'll want to get more than three marks on this question...
Explain two Buddhist beliefs about the Three Marks of Existence.
Include at least one example from Buddhist teaching.

[5]

Human Personality and Destiny | Buddhism

Different Buddhist branches have **different views** about **human nature** and the **ideal life**.

Theravada Buddhists **believe humans are made of** *Five Aggregates*

The **Five Aggregates** (**skandhas**) are the five **layers of experience** that make up the **human personality**:

1 FORM	**2 SENSATION**	**3 PERCEPTION**	**4 MENTAL FORMATIONS**	**5 CONSCIOUSNESS**
physical things that can be touched (e.g. seeing chocolate)	basic feelings towards something (e.g. I like chocolate)	recognising something (e.g. I know what chocolate is)	opinions about something (e.g. I think that chocolate is bad for me, so I will choose to not eat it)	awareness (e.g. I am in my house, sitting on the sofa, looking at chocolate)

- These five things are **constantly changing** (e.g. we are always experiencing different things), so the **human personality** is also constantly changing. This links with the Buddhist view that there is **no fixed self** (anatta).

- In the Khandha Sutta (a part of the Sutta Pitaka) the Five Aggregates are described as "**clinging aggregates**" because Buddhists believe that humans **cling** to these five things and this leads to **suffering**.

- Buddhists think we should try to **detach ourselves** from the Five Aggregates so that we can **suffer less**. The Buddha taught that these aggregates are **temporary**, as is the concept of 'self' — only when we realise this will we **end suffering** and **find enlightenment**.

> **Mahayana Buddhists** also believe that humans are made up of the **Five Aggregates**. They believe in the teaching of **sunyata** (emptiness). People are **empty** because they have **no fixed self** — they are made up of the **constantly changing** Five Aggregates.

Mahayana Buddhists **believe there's a potential Buddha** *inside us*

- Buddhists believe **all humans** have the potential to become **enlightened** — this is called **Buddha-nature**. A human being who has become **enlightened** (see p.30) and is **free of suffering** has reached **Buddhahood**.

- This is possible for **all humans**, but most **don't achieve it** because the road to Buddhahood is a lot of **hard work**. You need to become **generous**, **moral**, **patient**, **wise** and **energetic**, and have mastered **meditation** — this is known as the **Six Perfections** (see p.34).

> In the Abhidhamma Pitaka (49-52), it says that *"the well-instructed disciple"* can reach enlightenment.

- A **Bodhisattva** is someone who has followed the **Buddha's teachings** and reached **enlightenment**. They have achieved the **Six Perfections** and chosen to **stay on earth** to **help others** reach the **same destiny**. This is the **ideal goal** for a Mahayana Buddhist because **helping others** is important to them.

Pure Land Buddhists are a small group of Mahayana Buddhists who follow the teachings of **Amitabha Buddha**. They believe that Amitabha Buddha was a **king** who reached **Buddhahood** and created a **paradise land** where people can be **reborn** if they live a good life. Pure Land Buddhists' **ideal goal** is to be born into **Pure Land** so they can become **enlightened** (as this is not possible on earth).

Theravada Buddhists **believe in reaching enlightenment** *too*

- In **Theravada Buddhism**, an **arhat** is someone who has followed the **Buddha's teachings** and reached **enlightenment**. They no longer suffer because they have come to understand the **truth about life** and found **peace**.

- An arhat **will not be reborn** because they are free from the **cycle of rebirth** (see p.33). Unlike in Mahayana Buddhism, this is only possible by living a **monastic life**, which is free from **distractions** (e.g. Buddhist monks are celibate).

- Becoming an arhat is the **ideal goal** for Theravada Buddhists.

Five Aggregates, Six Perfections — that's a lot of numbers...

There's lots to remember on this page, so take some time to make sure it's all sunk in. Try closing the book, then see if you can write down the names of the Five Aggregates and what they mean.

Buddhism | # The Buddha's Life

Siddhartha Gautama (the Buddha) is the **most important figure** in Buddhism. This page is all about his life.

The Four Sights are the experiences that changed Siddhartha's life

- Siddhartha Gautama was a **rich prince** who lived **over 2 400 years ago** in **Nepal**. He lived a life of **luxury** with his wife and son. His father made sure that Siddhartha didn't have to **leave the palace grounds** so everything he needed was brought to the palace — he **never saw the outside world**.

- When Siddhartha turned 29, one of his servants took him on a trip **outside the palace grounds** and he saw the **outside world** for the first time. There were **four things** that **shocked him** and led him to **change** the way he lived:

> The story of Siddhartha's **Four Sights** is part of the **Jataka Tales**, which are a part of the **Sutta Pitaka**.

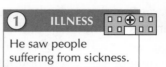
| ① ILLNESS |
| He saw people suffering from sickness. |

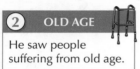
| ② OLD AGE |
| He saw people suffering from old age. |

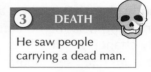
| ③ DEATH |
| He saw people carrying a dead man. |

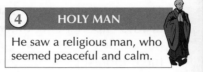
| ④ HOLY MAN |
| He saw a religious man, who seemed peaceful and calm. |

- These experiences made Siddhartha feel **anxious** because he knew that he would have to **suffer** just like the people he had seen.

Siddhartha decided to live an ascetic life

- Siddhartha was **inspired** by the holy man, who seemed **peaceful** and **calm**. Siddhartha decided he wanted to be **like this man**, so he **moved away** from the palace and found a **religious teacher** who taught him about **asceticism**.

- Siddhartha lived like this for **six years** and spent most of his time **meditating**. He grew very **thin** and only ate and drank enough to **survive**.

> **asceticism**
> *giving up pleasurable things (e.g. tasty food and drinks) and living a simple life*

Siddhartha became the Buddha

1 After **six years** of living an **ascetic life**, Siddhartha still didn't feel **peaceful** and **calm**. Instead he felt **frustrated** and was still **afraid** of **future suffering**. He realised that finding the **truth** about life would take a lot of **hard work** and he needed **physical nourishment** (not starvation) to support his task.

2 He decided to **give up** his life of asceticism and live in **moderation** (not in poverty or in riches). This is called the **Middle Way**.

> **"Avoiding these two extremes [asceticism and riches] leads to peace, direct knowledge..."** *Samyutta Nikaya 56.11*

3 Siddhartha still spent a lot of time **meditating**. One day, whilst meditating underneath the **Bodhi tree** (a fig tree in India), he reached **enlightenment**. This means he came to understand the true **meaning of life** (see p.30)

4 Siddhartha came to be called **the Buddha** because he was **enlightened**. He decided to spend the rest of his life **teaching others** how to do the same.

> "Buddha" means "enlightened one".

Take the time to practise spelling tricky words...

It's easy to misspell words like "asceticism", so spend some time memorising the spelling of any words you struggle with. Remember there are marks for SPaG in the longer 12 mark answers.

The Four Noble Truths

The Buddha's first lesson was about the Four Noble Truths. These are facts about life which can help people avoid suffering. They're written down in the Pali Canon in the Dhammacakkappavattana Sutta, Sutta Pitaka.

1) *Dukkha* means *suffering*

- Humans are **constantly suffering** for different reasons. Even **positive experiences** can lead to suffering because these experiences **don't last forever**, e.g. if you enjoyed your holiday to Spain, you might have felt sad when it was over.
- There are **three types** of suffering:

emotional and mental pain	suffering because of change	suffering because of attachment

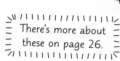 There's more about these on page 26.

2) *Samudaya* means *the cause* of suffering

- The **cause** (samudaya) of suffering is **craving** (tanha). Humans suffer because they are always **craving something**.
- There are **three types** of craving:

Sensual Craving	**Craving for the self**	**Craving to avoid suffering**
 wanting food, sleep, water etc.	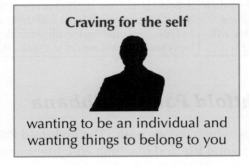 wanting to be an individual and wanting things to belong to you	 not wanting to do things that cause pain

- All craving is caused by the **Three Poisons** — these are represented as a **pig**, a **rooster** and a **snake** in Buddhist art:

IGNORANCE

Ignorance means **not knowing** about something. Ignorance leads to **craving**, e.g. if you don't understand that **attachment** to things won't make you **happy**, then you will crave a big house and great car and not know any better. This is an example of **craving for the self**.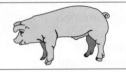

GREED

Being greedy means you want **too much** of something, e.g. greediness might lead me to have a **sensual craving** for cake.

HATE

Feelings of hate often lead to **cravings**, e.g. hate for another person might lead to a craving to **avoid suffering** because I might want to avoid that person.

- **Craving** leads to **suffering** because we can **never really have** what we are craving — this is because everything is **impermanent** (anicca). For example, a greed for cake will **never** be satisfied because the experience of eating cake will be **temporary** — people will always be left wanting **more cake**.

3) Nibbana *is the absence of suffering*

- The **ultimate goal** of Buddhism is to reach **nibbana** (also spelt "nirvana"). nibbana is a **calm and peaceful state**, which is **free from suffering**.

- In order to reach nibbana, a Buddhist must become **enlightened**. This means they must understand that all **craving** leads to **suffering** and so suffering will stop when craving stops. The Buddha taught that to stop craving things, a person needs to stop being **ignorant**, **greedy** and **hateful** (the **Three Poisons**) because these three things cause **all cravings**.

> This is only possible if a person stops **attaching themselves** to things, e.g. you could stop being attached to your phone by using it less, so you stop wanting to use it so much.

- The word **nibbana** literally means **blowing out** or **extinguishing**. This is because a Buddhist only reaches nibbana when the **Three Poisons** have been **extinguished**. Once this happens, a Buddhist will **stop craving** things and will then **stop suffering**.

> This process is sometimes called the **cessation of suffering** (nirodha).

- Buddhist **traditions** view enlightenment and nibbana **differently**:

THERAVADA	MAHAYANA	PURE LAND
Enlightenment is only possible in a **monastic life** (living as a monk) because there are **few distractions**, e.g. it might be easier for a monk not to crave cake because they never eat cake or sugary foods.	Enlightenment is possible through the **Middle Way**. This means not living with riches, but also not living in poverty. (This is based on the story of how Siddhartha became the Buddha by giving up a life of ascetism — see p.28).	Enlightenment is only possible in the **Pure Land** (after death). On Earth there are **too many distractions** to reach enlightenment.
An **arhat** (see p.27) is concerned with their **own nibbana**. They are not dedicated to teaching others about this. After an arhat dies, they will be **free** from the **cycle of rebirth** (see p.33)	A Bodhisattva (see p.27) chooses to teach others about the path to nibbana and dedicate their life to reducing suffering for all. After death, they will be reborn into the world to continue this task.	Once a Buddhist has reached nibbana in the **Pure Land**, they are released from the **cycle of rebirth**.

4) Magga *is the Eightfold Path to nibbana*

- The fourth noble truth is **magga**, which means **path**. The **Eightfold Path** provides eight **rules** for living a **good life** and reaching **enlightenment**. This path is often represented as a **wheel** with **eight spokes**.

- The **Threefold Way** describes the three **sections** of this path. These are **ethics** (sila), **meditation** (samadhi) and **wisdom** (panna).

> "The Four Noble Truths — suffering, the cause of suffering, the cessation of suffering, and the Noble Eightfold Path leading to the cessation of suffering."
> *Dhammapada 190-191*

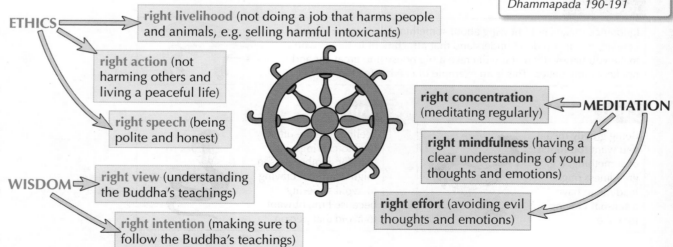

ETHICS

right livelihood (not doing a job that harms people and animals, e.g. selling harmful intoxicants)

right action (not harming others and living a peaceful life)

right speech (being polite and honest)

WISDOM

right view (understanding the Buddha's teachings)

right intention (making sure to follow the Buddha's teachings)

right concentration (meditating regularly) MEDITATION

right mindfulness (having a clear understanding of your thoughts and emotions)

right effort (avoiding evil thoughts and emotions)

REVISION TASK

Reaching nibbana isn't meant to be easy...

Drawing diagrams can really help with your revision. Try drawing your own version of the Eightfold Path diagram above — make sure you divide the diagram clearly into three sections.

Places of Worship and Ritual — Buddhism

Buddhists **pay respect** to the **Buddha** and take part in **rituals** both in **religious buildings** and **at home**.

A temple is a religious building in Buddhism

Temples are designed to be **peaceful** and **calm** places.
Buddhists go to the temple for **various reasons**:

- to **meditate** — there is usually a room to do this in called the **meditation hall** or **gompas**
- to **chant**
- to listen to a **sutra** (teaching from Buddhist scripture)
- to visit the **shrine room**

SHRINE ROOMS

- All temples have a **shrine room** with a **statue** of the Buddha (**Buddha rupa**).
- Visitors to the shrine room leave **gifts**, such as food, water, candles (which represent enlightenment), flowers and incense, in order to show **gratitude** to the Buddha.
- Buddhists enter the room with **bare feet** as a sign of **respect**, and sometimes **sing** or **chant** to the statue to show **devotion**. **Theravada Buddhists** often wear **white** when visiting this room to show **commitment** to the **non-self** (anatta).
- Some Buddhists also have shrine rooms inside their **own houses**. These will include a **Buddha rupa**, which is often placed on a **high shelf** with nothing above it to show the Buddha's **importance**.
- Buddhists at home or in the temple can use the **Buddha rupa** as a **focus for meditation**, e.g. they can concentrate on the Buddha's **qualities** and aim to develop these qualities in **themselves**.

> The Buddha is one of the **Three Jewels of Buddhism** (see p.25), so it's important to Buddhists to **pay respect** and **show thanks** for his teachings.

A monastery (viharas) is a place where monks and nuns live

- Buddhist monks and nuns usually lead an **ascetic life** (see p.28).
- Monasteries often have **halls of learning** (**gompas**) attached to them, where Buddhists can go to **learn more** about Buddhism and the Buddha's teachings.
- Monasteries are often in **isolated locations**, away from **distractions**, and are usually **self-sufficient** (they grow their own food).

> **monk / nun**
> *someone who lives in a monastery and devotes their life to a particular religion*

Buddhists take part in devotional ritual (puja)

- **Puja** is a **set of actions** that show **devotion** to the Buddha. Buddhists do this to say **thank you** to the Buddha for his teachings.
- Puja can be a **ceremonial occasion** (this means it's a **public event** that lots of people do together) or it can take place **at home**. Puja can include:

> **ritual**
> *a sequence of actions*

> **artefact**
> *a man-made object*

| **chanting** (speaking or singing words or sounds continually) | **mantras** (speaking or singing sacred words) — Buddhists believe these have a **calming effect** on people. They are something written on **paper** and stored in a **prayer wheel**. |

| **meditation** (see p.26) | using **malas** (a string of beads, which Buddhists move through their fingers to guide **chanting** or **meditation**) | leaving **gifts** for the **Buddha rupa** |

> Buddhists use various artefacts when taking part in rituals, e.g. Buddha rupas, malas and prayer wheels.

Don't forget there are differences between the Buddhist branches...

Puja is different in different Buddhist traditions. For example, a large part of puja for Pure Land Buddhists is chanting the name of Amitabha (see p.27) in an attempt to reduce daily suffering and show devotion.

Buddhism	# Meditation

There are lots of different **meditation practices** within Buddhism. This page tells you all about the **main ones**.

There are *different kinds of meditation*

- Buddhists meditate to feel **calm** and **peaceful** so they can slowly come to realise the **truth about life** (the Three Marks of Existence — see page 26). Eventually, not necessarily in this lifetime, this will lead to **enlightenment**.
- Some Buddhists go to **meditation retreats**. This involves **going away** for a period of time to live with other Buddhists and taking part in **daily meditation**.
- There are various **meditation practices** within Buddhism:

Samatha **means** *calm meditation*

- The **aim** of samatha is to find **peacefulness**.
- Buddhists practising samatha sit in a **comfortable position** (e.g. cross-legged or on a chair) and try to focus their mind on **one single thing**. This can be an **object** (e.g. a lit candle) or it can be the **process of breathing**.
- By focusing on only one thing, the mind will become **clear** and free from **thoughts**, **feelings** and **worries**.

> **"If with a pure mind a person speaks or acts happiness follows"** *Dhammapada 2*

 Focusing on **breathing** during meditation is called the **mindfulness of breath** and it includes practices such as **counting** the number of breaths or making breaths **longer**.

Vipassana **means** *seeing the truth*

Once a Buddhist is comfortable with samatha, they can move on to **vipassana meditation**.

- The aim of vipassana is to use meditation to come to realise the **Three Marks of Existence** and then to extinguish **the Three Poisons** (see p.29).
- Instead of focusing the mind on one particular thing, vipassana meditation involves observing the **mind**, **body** and **world**. This can include observing the **thoughts**, **feelings** and **worries** that come into the mind and **acknowledging their existence**.
- Buddhists believe that through observing the mind they will come to realise the **truth about our existence** — everything **suffers**, everything is **impermanent** and there is **no fixed self**.
- Vipassana meditation can involve **sitting** or **walking**.

> **Zen Buddhists** take part in a version of vipassana called **zazen**. Zazen meditation focuses on being in the **present moment** (not thinking about the past or future) and involves **sitting**. The aim of zazen is to appreciate that there is **no fixed self**. Zen Buddhists often take part in zazen for **hours** at a time.

Some Buddhists use **visualisation** *to aid meditation*

Visualisation involves holding an **image** in the mind. Buddhists might look at a particular image first and then try to **imagine** that image in their minds and use it as a **point of focus** during meditation.

> **Tibetan Buddhists** visualise images of people who have **reached nibbana**. They call these people **deities** and try to focus on their **characteristics** in order to bring out these characteristics in **themselves**.

> **Mahayana Buddhists** might visualise a being who has become **enlightened** — a **Buddha** or a **Bodhisattva** (see p.27).

> Other Buddhists visualise an **enlightened version** of themselves.

Take a deep breath, then try this exam-style question...
Give two examples of Buddhist meditation practices. [2]

Ethical Teaching — Buddhism

There are plenty of **new terms** to learn on this page, so make sure you read it **carefully** and **understand** it all.

Buddhists believe in a cycle of rebirth (samsara)

- Buddhists believe in **rebirth**. This means that after death a person's energy continues in a **new life**. The cycle of rebirth is called samsara (meaning around and around) because it will not end until a person finds **enlightenment** and reaches **nibbana**. Samsara is often represented by a **wheel**.

- The energy that passes on into a new life is **karmic energy**. Karma means **action**. Buddhists believe that all actions (good and bad) have **consequences**. The **karmic energy** a person produces in their life will affect the **new life** they are born into.

> "If with an impure mind someone speaks or acts, suffering follows."
> *Dhammapada 1*

Buddhists believe in six realms of existence

God realm	The gods live **luxurious lives** of pleasure and happiness, but they don't see other **suffering** so remain **ignorant**.
Demi-god realm	Demi-gods are **jealous** and **hateful** beings.
Human realm	The human realm offers the opportunity to find **enlightenment** and **freedom** from the **cycle of rebirth**.
Animal realm	Animals live a life motivated by **greed** and **impulse**.
Hungry ghost realm	Hungry ghosts are **never satisfied**. They are constantly in a state of **wanting**.
Demon realm	The hell realm is the **worst realm** to be born into because it is filled with **pain**.

A person's **actions** will affect the realm of existence they are **reborn** into, e.g. someone obsessed with **money** might be reborn into the **hungry ghosts** realm, where their **greed** will never be satisfied.

- Some Buddhists believe the six realms are **physical** (e.g. being born into the **animal realm** means being born **as an animal**).
- Others see them as **metaphors** to describe **states of mind** (e.g. being born into the animal realm means being born into a human life but **acting like an animal**).

Karuna means compassion

compassion
concern for the suffering of others

Showing **compassion** produces **good karma** — Buddhists do this in a variety of ways, e.g. providing **food** for the **poor** or releasing **caged animals**.

Compassion is particularly important in **Mahayana Buddhism** because once a **Bodhisattva** has achieved wisdom, they will feel compassion towards those trapped in the **cycle of rebirth** and try to **help them**.

In **Theravada Buddhism**, Karuna is one of the **Four Sublime States** (compassion, loving kindness, calmness and sympathy) which show how Buddhists should **treat others**.

> "If we are to protect this home of ours, each of us needs to experience a vivid sense of universal altruism"
> *Dalai Lama (Head of Tibetan Buddhism)*

Metta means loving kindness

- **Loving kindness** (metta) is a state of mind that wishes **happiness** to all. There are **five stages**:

1	2	3	4	5
feeling peace **within yourself** (getting rid of feelings of self-hatred)	wishing peace and happiness to **friends** (letting go of any jealousy you might feel)	neutralising feelings towards **acquaintances** (letting go of any judgement towards people we see or meet)	neutralising feelings towards **people we dislike** (letting go of dislike and wishing happiness on these people)	wishing happiness to **all**

> "May all beings be happy and secure, may they have happy minds" *Metta Sutta, Sutta Pitaka*

- Buddhists try to achieve this state by practising **meditation** and repeating phrases from the Metta Sutta, a part of the **Pali Canon**.

EXAM TIP

Compassion and loving kindness are central to Buddhism...

If you don't know the answer to a 1 mark multiple choice question, start by discounting answers that you know are wrong. Then, have a guess — you won't lose marks and you might get lucky.

Buddhism | # Precepts and Perfections

If you thought you were done with numbers, think again — there are **5 precepts** and **6 perfections** to learn.

The Five Moral Precepts are guidance *about how to live life*

- Unlike in other religions, there are **no absolute rules** or **commandments** in Buddhism. Instead, the Five Moral Precepts are a list of things Buddhists should **avoid doing**. Avoiding these things produces **good karma**, but doing any of these things produces **negative karma**.

- The five precepts aim to reduce the amount of **suffering** in the world. Different Buddhists follow these precepts to **different degrees**. A Buddhist **monk** or **nun** may be able to follow these rules all the time, whereas others may **struggle** to do this, e.g. in everyday life it might be necessary to tell a small lie in order to avoid hurting someone's feelings.

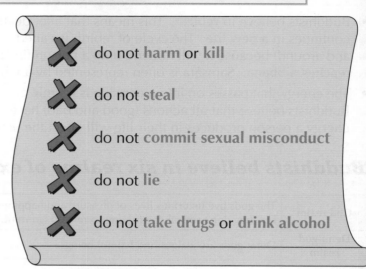

✗ do not **harm** or **kill**

✗ do not **steal**

✗ do not **commit sexual misconduct**

✗ do not **lie**

✗ do not **take drugs** or **drink alcohol**

Mahayana Buddhists aspire to have *Six Perfections*

The **Six Perfections** of the **Mahayana tradition** are **six characteristics** that you must have to become **enlightened**. These can be found in Mahayana **sacred texts** in the **Lotus Sutra** and the **Large Sutra**.

GENEROSITY:
Being **generous** means being **willing to give** to others. In the Mahayana tradition, Buddhists are encouraged to **help others** with their path to **enlightenment** and to show **metta** and **karuna** at all times. Behaviour must be **selfless**, e.g. giving food to the poor because it makes you feel good would not count as a generous act.

MORALITY:
Being **moral** means following the **Dhamma** (see p.25). This includes living life by the **Five Moral Precepts**.

PATIENCE:
Being **patient** means accepting the **suffering** of life and being **kind** and **tolerant** towards those around you.

ENERGY:
An **energetic** Buddhist shows complete **dedication** to **enlightenment**. This includes overcoming **obstacles** on the way — not giving up when things get tricky. Once enlightenment has been found, this energy can be dedicated to **helping others** find it.

MEDITATION:
To become **enlightened**, a Buddhist must have **mastered meditation** (see p.32).

WISDOM:
Wisdom can only be achieved by developing the **five previous perfections**. Wisdom means a true understanding of **anatta** (see p.26). Buddhists sometimes refer to anatta as **emptiness** — understanding that all existence is empty and there is **no fixed self**.

Learn all this and you'll be on your way to exam perfection...
Make a mind map that names the Six Perfections and describes each one. Add some colour to help you remember them — you could even sketch some quick doodles if you find this helps.

Beliefs, Teachings and Practices — Buddhism

Rituals and Festivals

Buddhist communities celebrate things differently, but almost all Buddhists take part in some form of **ritual** when somebody **dies**. Make sure you know about the key Buddhist **rituals** and **festivals** on this page.

Theravada *Buddhists cremate the bodies of the dead*

- Before the cremation takes place, Theravada Buddhists usually take part in a **service** led by a **monk**, who reminds the mourners about impermanence (anicca).
- Mourners will usually display an **image** of the person who has died — it is believed this produces good karma for the person.
- Various forms of merit making take place before and after the body is cremated:

> Death rituals (in all Buddhist traditions) often involve activities that aim to increase good karma for the dead. This is known as merit making.

filling up a jug of water to represent good karma	leaving offerings (e.g. flowers or food) at monasteries on behalf of the dead person	preaching for the benefit of the dead (monks visit the dead person's house regularly to speak about anicca)

Mahayana *death traditions vary in different countries*

In Japan, once someone has died, Buddhists leave **flowers**, **candles** and **incense** next to their body. These things represent **impermanence** (anicca) and are burned with the body. The body will be prepared for cremation by being **washed** and **dressed** by mourners. A Buddhist priest will usually read from a **sacred text** before the cremation. Afterwards the ashes will be placed in an **urn** and **buried**.

Pure Land Buddhists place the **head** of the dead person facing towards the **west**, where some believe the Pure Land is.

In **Tibet**, Buddhists believe that the dead must pass through **bardo** before they are reborn. For some, bardo can be a **painful experience** and so Buddhists read the Tibetan **Book of the Dead** to the deceased as they believe it helps them pass through. Due to the **terrain** in Tibet (mountainous), there are not many good places to bury people and so bodies are usually **cremated** or left at the **top of a hill** for birds to eat — this is called a **sky burial**.

Wesak *celebrates the Buddha's birth, enlightenment and death*

Most Buddhists take part in **Wesak**, as it is an opportunity to celebrate the **life** and **death** of **Siddhartha Gautama**. Buddhist communities mark the festival differently, but traditional practices include:

- providing **offerings** to monasteries (e.g. food, clothes, flowers)
- **bathing** of the Buddha (washing statues of the Buddha)
- chanting the **Five Moral Precepts**
- listening to **scripture** about the Buddha's enlightenment (Avatamsaka Sutra, Pali Canon)
- releasing **caged animals** (to represent compassion)
- **meditating**
- singing **traditional songs**

In some Asian countries, large **processions** take place where people **dress up** and hold **lanterns** to celebrate Wesak. In Great Britain, the festival is a chance to come together as a **Buddhist community** and celebration tends to take place within the **temple**.

Parinirvana *is the last stage of nibbana*

- **Parinirvana Day** is a **Mahayana** day of celebration that marks the **Buddha's death**.
- After the Buddha died, he reached the **last stage of nibbana** and was free from the **cycle of rebirth** (see p.33). Mahayana Buddhists celebrate this day by taking part in a **special puja** (see p.31), which includes listening to passages from the **Nirvana Sutra** (part of the Mahayana's collection of sacred sutra).
- Buddhists visit temples and take part in **meditation**. Some Buddhists also go on **pilgrimages** to visit the Buddha's place of death (Kushinagar, India) during this time.

Most Buddhist rituals and festivals are focused on death...

Death is important to Buddhists because it reminds them of impermanence (anicca). Festivals like Parinirvana Day offer Buddhists a chance to reflect on impermanence and their own path to enlightenment.

Revision Summary

There was a lot in that section, so now it's your chance to find out how much you **remember**. These are **exam-style questions**, so you can get an idea of how **long** and **detailed** your answers have to be. If you're **stuck** on anything, **go back** to the relevant page in the section and then **try** the question **again**.

We'll start off with some straightforward 1 mark multiple choice questions.

1) Which of the following describes the layers of experience that make up the human personality?
   a) The Three Jewels of Buddhism   b) The Five Aggregates
   c) The Three Marks of Existence   d) The Five Moral Precepts

2) Which of the following is a set of actions designed to show devotion to the Buddha?
   a) Anicca   b) Puja   c) Dependent Arising   d) Buddha rupa

3) Which of the following is the cycle of rebirth?
   a) Magga   b) Vipassana   c) Samsara   d) Karma

4) Which of the following is the concept of loving kindness?
   a) Metta   b) Wesak   c) Samudaya   d) Nibbana

These questions are worth 2 marks. You need to make two brief points in your answer.

5) Name two of the Three Poisons.

6) Name two of the sections that make up the Threefold Way.

7) Name two of the Six Realms of Existence.

8) Name two of the Six Perfections in Mahayana Buddhism.

These are 4 mark questions. To get full marks, you need to develop the points you make.

9) Explain two ways in which belief in anicca (impermanence) might influence Buddhists today.

10) Explain two contrasting Buddhist understandings of nibbana and enlightenment.

11) Explain two ways in which the Five Moral Precepts might influence Buddhists today.

12) Explain two contrasting ways of commemorating a person's death in Buddhism.

These questions are worth 5 marks, so you need to develop and explain your answer. You also need to include Buddhist teachings in your answer.

Your points need to be nice and clear in the longer answer questions. Make sure your writing is well organised.

13) Explain two Buddhist ideas about suffering.

14) Explain two reasons why the story of the Buddha's life is important for Buddhists.

15) Explain two Buddhist ideas about rebirth.

16) Explain two reasons why helping others is important for Buddhists.

And the big one — this is a 12 mark question. Use the bullet point list below to help you plan your answer — the list gives you the things you need to include. Try coming up with arguments for and against the statement before you start, so you don't leave anything out.

17) 'Mastering the art of meditation is the most important thing a Buddhist can do to achieve enlightenment.' Evaluate this statement. Your answer should include the following:

   • examples from Buddhist teachings

   • arguments that support the statement

   There's advice on writing essays in the 'Do Well in Your Exam' section.

   • arguments that disagree with the statement

   • a conclusion

Beliefs, Teachings and Practices — Buddhism

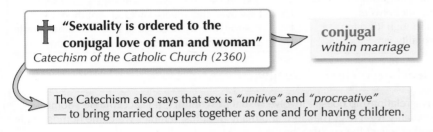

Sexuality and Sexual Relationships

Christianity & Buddhism

You must be aware of **religious** and **non-religious** views in Britain, and be able to give **two** or more contrasting religious views on **homosexuality** and **sex before marriage**, with at least one being **Christian**.

Some Christians believe that pre-marital sex is wrong

Traditionally, Christianity teaches that the only correct context for sexual activity is within marriage — sex outside of it is seen as a sin. This means cohabitation (living together unmarried) isn't approved of.

✝ **"Sexuality is ordered to the conjugal love of man and woman"**
Catechism of the Catholic Church (2360)

→ conjugal
within marriage

The Catechism also says that sex is *"unitive"* and *"procreative"* — to bring married couples together as one and for having children.

- Christians are urged to keep sex within marriage for positive reasons as well — marriage is believed to make sex more special. Both Christianity and Buddhism stress the importance of enjoying sex — the Song of Solomon in the Bible contains poems celebrating sexual desire and relationships.
- 'Strict' Christians think the principle of only having sex within marriage still applies. More liberal Christians might see this as outdated, although they still tend to see marriage as the ideal.

Sex outside of marriage is considered normal in British society

- Many British people think promiscuity is acceptable, especially now contraception (see p.39) is widely available — though a large number of sexual partners is seen more negatively.
- Humanists accept sex outside of marriage as long as it causes no harm to anyone. Atheists tend to accept it too.

Buddhists don't believe pre-marital sex is wrong

Sex itself is **not** seen as **sinful** in Buddhism, but sex can involve **craving** and **jealousy**, which cause **suffering** (dukkha). Buddhists will try to make sure their sexual relationships are **honest**, **loving** and **kind** so they don't create suffering.	The **Five Moral Precepts** (see p.34) teach Buddhists not to commit **sexual misconduct**, e.g. to not be **promiscuous** (having multiple sexual partners) as this could lead to **suffering**. Christians **agree** that promiscuity is wrong.	**Monks** and **nuns** living in **monasteries** abstain from sex because it is a form of **desire** and they believe all desire leads to **suffering** (dukkha).

Cohabitation is common within Buddhism

Buddhists do not always choose to get **married** because marriage is **not an important part** of the religion.

→ Cohabiting with someone else is **normal** and **acceptable**.

Christianity & Buddhism	**Sexuality and Sexual Relationships**

Homosexuality is a disputed topic

✝ **"Under no circumstances can [homosexual acts] be approved"** *Catechism of the Catholic Church (2357)*

The Christian scriptures seem to say that homosexual sex is wrong.

- The texts don't condemn people who have homosexual feelings but don't act upon them. This means some people who are homosexual and religious opt for celibacy (they don't have sexual relationships).
- They only condemn sex between men, not between women, which is hardly mentioned. (Though it's often frowned upon because male homosexuality is.)

Some Christians use the story of **Sodom** (Genesis 19:3-25) to argue against homosexuality.
- The city's destroyed after the men in Sodom demand sex with two **male angels** God sent.
- However, the angels say God sent them to destroy the city because of sin... so some people argue that God was going to destroy it anyway.

The Buddha did not give any **specific teaching** on homosexuality:

- Many Buddhists believe that as long as a relationship doesn't involve **sexual misconduct**, it is **acceptable**. Some Buddhist countries have made homosexuality **legal** (e.g. Thailand) and many Buddhist Temples welcome homosexuals.
- Buddhists' views on homosexuality tend to reflect the **country** they live in. Many Buddhist countries are **not accepting** of homosexuality, e.g. homosexuals in Tibet experience discrimination.

Homosexuality is considered normal in British society

The first same-sex marriages in the UK took place in 2014.

Even many religious people argue that, as the scriptures were written in a different **cultural context** from ours, we can't apply their standards today. Generally, the religions **condemn homophobia** and they're becoming more accepting of homosexuality.

Religious views on same-sex marriage can vary

	👍 **Views and actions IN FAVOUR of same-sex marriage**	👎 **Views and actions AGAINST same-sex marriage**
CHRISTIANITY	• Some Church of England clergy hold blessings for same-sex couples after they marry in civil (non-religious) ceremonies. • Anglican supporters of same-sex marriage say Christians should be loving to all and should support anyone who wants to marry. • Members of the congregation (particularly younger people) within the Catholic Church and the Church of England tend to be more likely to be in favour of same-sex marriage than their church leaders.	• The decision to legalise same-sex marriage in the UK was criticised by the Catholic Church and the Church of England. Many members of the clergy are against it. *The Catholic Church is strongly against homosexual relationships and same-sex marriage.* **"The Church of England affirms, according to our Lord's teaching, that marriage is ... a union... of one man with one woman."** *Canon B30* • Those in the Anglican church who are against same-sex marriage say it's a sin. • Many Christians believe it's wrong because one purpose of marriage is having children.
BUDDHISM	• Many Buddhists support same-sex marriage as long as the relationship is based on love and avoids suffering and sexual misconduct. • Some Buddhist temples hold blessings for same-sex marriages — e.g. the Buddhist Church of San Francisco performed its first same-sex marriage ceremony in the 1970s.	• Same-sex marriage is illegal in some predominantly Buddhist countries, e.g. Sri Lanka. • Some Buddhists view homosexual sex as sexual misconduct (one of the Five Moral Precepts), so they think same-sex marriage is wrong.

EXAM TIP

Views on homosexuality have changed over time...

Different religions have different views on this topic, but remember there are also different views within each religion. You often have to give two views in the exam and you get marks for detail.

Theme A — Relationships and Families

Contraception

You need to learn about the **contrasting** religious views on **contraception**.

Contraception prevents a woman becoming pregnant

Contraception is also known as birth control and is used to **stop** a woman **conceiving**. There are **two types**:

1 Temporary
e.g. the contraceptive pill or condoms

2 Permanent (also called **sterilisation**)
e.g. a vasectomy

Using contraception is sometimes called 'family planning'.

Most **atheists** and **humanists** have no objection to contraception:

They think it's better if people only have children if they really **want** them.

Contraception allows people to **choose** when to have sex, by limiting the risk of pregnancy.

Some types also reduce the risk of **STIs** (sexually transmitted infections).

Both religions have a range of views about contraception

The table below **summarises** the main Christian and Buddhist arguments **for** and **against** contraception:

Views IN FAVOUR of contraception	Views AGAINST contraception
CHRISTIANITY • Some Roman Catholics are highly in favour of contraception because of concerns about **STIs**. • The Anglican, Methodist and Presbyterian Churches are in favour of contraception, suggesting that it lets parents **plan** their family in a **responsible** way. • Many Christians believe that contraception should be a question of **individual conscience**. They see it as positive that women can **control** when they get pregnant.	• The Catechism of the Catholic Church 2367 says that married couples should *"transmit human life"* (i.e. have children). • Humanae Vitae 14 says that anything *"deliberately contraceptive"* is *"intrinsically wrong"*. • The Church says contraception may lead to **promiscuity**. • Some Christians object to forms of contraception that might destroy a fertilised egg, such as the morning after pill — this is because they see it as being the same as **abortion**.
• The Catholic Church does allow **natural** contraception — only having sex at the **less fertile** times in a woman's menstrual cycle. • Christians are divided over sterilisation, which prevents people ever having children.	
BUDDHISM • Many Buddhists are in favour of contraception as long as it is used with the **right intention** (see p.30), e.g. controlling the spread of **STIs** or if having a baby would cause the **mother to suffer**. • Unlike Christianity, Buddhists do **not** believe having children is a **religious duty**. Buddhists would see using contraception for family planning as a **right intention**.	• Buddhists believe that it is always **wrong** to **harm** or **kill** a **living thing** (see p.34), so, similarly to Christians, some Buddhists object to contraception that destroys a **fertilised egg**, e.g. the morning after pill. • Having sex for **pleasure** alone shows sensual **craving** (see p.29). All craving leads to **suffering**, so some Buddhists might see sex for pleasure as a **distraction** from the path to enlightenment.

Remember that Christian views focus on marital sex...

Have a go at this exam-style question using the information you've learnt on this page.
Explain two contrasting religious beliefs about contraception.

[4]

Theme A — Relationships and Families

General, Christianity & Buddhism	# Marriage and Divorce

Christians see marriage as a **sacred duty**, but for Buddhists it's a **personal choice**.

Marriage *in the UK — things have* changed

Non-religious attitudes to **marriage**, **divorce** and **cohabitation** are very different now to in the past.

Marriage

- The number of marriages taking place in the UK each year has been **decreasing** over the last **40 years**.
- Although many **non-religious** people still see marriage as **important**, others see it as **unnecessary**.
- People are also tending to get married **later** in life, and many people have **children** without being married.
- **Same-sex marriages** are now **legal** across the UK. Many people think this is good because it creates **equality**.

Cohabitation

- It's now more **common** (and **acceptable**) for people to cohabit (**live together**) — either **before** marrying or **instead of** getting married.
- Cohabiting couples don't have the same **legal rights** as married ones though.

Divorce

- Divorce has become far more **common**. **Non-religious** people often see it as **sensible** if the couple don't get on, as they'll be **happier** if they divorce.
- Some argue parents fighting can **harm** children more than divorce.
- However, many **religious** people try to **avoid** divorce if at all possible.

Christians and *Buddhists* *have different views about* marriage

- The views of many Christians on **marriage** and **divorce** have **changed less** over the last few decades than those of **wider British society**. This is because, for Christians, marriage reflects the **union** of **Jesus** with his **followers**.

- Buddhists do not see marriage as a **sacred duty**. Marriage is a **personal choice** and seen as more of a **social contract**. **Weddings** are usually **secular** ceremonies, but sometimes couples go to a **monastery** to receive a **blessing** from a monk afterwards.

- Some Buddhists believe **enlightenment** is not possible within a marriage because being **attached** to another person can cause **suffering**. Theravada monks, for example, remain **celibate** and **do not marry**.

- The **Sigalovada Sutta** offers simple **guidance** on how to treat your partner in marriage.
- It encourages both partners to be **respectful** and **faithful** to one another.
- It also provides guidance about **gender roles** within marriage (e.g. women should take on responsibility of the household and men should provide women with the money to buy things).
- Nowadays, some Buddhists might view this guidance as **outdated**.

Christians and Buddhists have some similar *and some* different *views*

Purpose of marriage

In Christianity, marriage is a **covenant** (contract) between **two** people to offer **love**, **support** and **commitment**, and to have **children**.

For most Buddhists, the purpose of marriage is to have **children** and form a **loving partnership**. Marriage is not a religious contract, but a **secular** one.

Polygamy

Nearly all Christians see polygamy (marriage to **multiple** people) as **wrong**.

There is **no specific** Buddhist **teaching** on polygamy, but Buddhists believe that being **greedy** is a hindrance to reaching **enlightenment**, so they might see having more than one partner as **unacceptable**.

Adultery

Faithfulness in marriage is important — adultery is forbidden in the **Ten Commandments** (Exodus 20:14).

Buddhists aim to **avoid suffering** as much as possible. The **Five Moral Precepts** also teach Buddhists to avoid **sexual misconduct**.

Marriage and Divorce

Religious views on cohabitation vary

Some Christians, including the Catholic Church, tend to be **against** cohabitation — they disagree with sex outside marriage.

Many Christians accept cohabitation, especially as **preparation** for **marriage**. Pope Francis has recognised it can be hard for people to marry, e.g. for financial reasons — but they should be **encouraged** to **marry** eventually.

It is common for Buddhists to cohabitate, as marriage is **not an important part** of Buddhism. Many Buddhists choose to **never get married** and enjoy raising a family in cohabitation.

In a book called 'Not Just Good, but Beautiful', Pope Francis said marriage is 'indispensable' to society.

Different **Christian Churches have** varying attitudes **to divorce**

There are different views as to whether divorce is permissible, or even possible.

Impossible

The **Roman Catholic Church** says it's impossible to divorce (Catechism of the Catholic Church 2382). Marriage is a **sacrament** — God made the couple one flesh, which can't be undone. However, a marriage can be **annulled** (declared void) if the couple never had sex or if a partner didn't consent to or understand the marriage, or refused to have children.

Possible ✓

- The **Church of England** says divorce is possible and accepts that some marriages fail. Divorcees can usually **re-marry in church**.
- **Nonconformist** Churches (e.g. Baptists and Methodists) will usually **re-marry** divorcees.

Some members of these Churches disagree with this, and individual ministers may not be willing to re-marry divorcees if it goes against their conscience.

- Jesus himself was generally anti-divorce. In Matthew 19:8-9 NIV, he says divorce and remarriage are only allowed if someone's partner's been unfaithful.
- Some Christians view an **unhappy** marriage as a **waste** of two lives, and so see divorce as preferable.

"A man [and] his wife ... will become one flesh. ... what God has joined together, let no one separate." *Mark 10:7-9 NIV*

There are no rules **against** divorce **in Buddhism**

- Divorce is seen as a **last resort** for Buddhists. The couple will often try to make the marriage work with the help of their **family** and **community**. If the marriage is still causing **suffering** then it is seen as **unhealthy** to hold onto this attachment, and most Buddhists would agree that divorcing is the most **compassionate** thing.
- It is important not to cause **more suffering** during the divorce process, so Buddhists will try to follow the **Five Moral Precepts** and use **love** and **compassion**.

Phew, what a lot of different opinions...

In the exam, you might be asked to give similar or contrasting beliefs about marriage and divorce — try comparing Christian and Buddhist views so you understand the differences and similarities.

Christianity & Buddhism

Families

As the saying goes, 'you can choose your GCSEs, but you can't choose your family'. Or something like that...

Family *is important* to Christians and most *Buddhists*

- Ideally, a **stable** family can give a child a sense of **identity** and a feeling of **security**. They'll learn how to **behave**, how to give and receive **love**, and about **right** and **wrong**.
- Many Christians think it's best for a child to have a **father** and a **mother** present (ideally the child's **biological** parents), so that they grow up with one **role model** of each sex.
- For Christians, ideally, the couple would be **married**, as it's believed this provides more **stability**, but for Buddhists living in **cohabitation** is an **acceptable** and normal way to raise a child.
- For Buddhists, there are **no rules** about family life — families try to live happily together in a way that doesn't create **suffering**. Many Buddhists live in **extended families** (e.g. with grandparents), which is different to the way many British families live.
- For **religious** people, family life can be a way of introducing their **children** to their **faith**. The table shows some of the ways Christians and Buddhists **link** family life and faith:

	CHRISTIANITY	BUDDHISM
Purpose of family life	Family life is **important** for most Christians. It's seen as a way to build a **stable society**. "family is 'the first and vital cell of society'." *Pope John Paul II, Familiaris Consortio 42 (Catholic teachings on family)* Festivals such as Christmas and Easter have a strong emphasis on **celebration** within the **family**.	Buddhism is not a particularly **family-centred** religion. Buddhist monks and nuns choose to **detach themselves** from their families in order to find **enlightenment**. For many other Buddhists, family is **important**. Buddhist families visit **temples** together and take part in **puja** together.
Educating children in the faith at home	Many Christians believe it's important to have **children** and **educate** them in the **faith** — see for example Catechism of the Catholic Church 2226 and this quote: "bring [your children] up in the training and instruction of the Lord." *Ephesians 6:4 NIV* This might include activities at home such as reading the child Bible **stories**, or teaching them about **prayer** by **saying grace** (giving thanks) before meals.	Buddhists believe that parents have a duty to guide a child towards *"good actions"* and help them avoid *"wrongdoing"* (Sigalovada Sutta). For many Buddhists, this can be achieved through **educating** a child about their faith. In the home, many Buddhists have a **shrine** and take part in daily **puja** (see p.31) and **meditation** as a family.
Educating children in the faith outside the home	Many churches offer **help** in raising children, through **Sunday schools**. These schools aim to teach Christian **morals** and **ideals** through the study of **Bible stories**.	Buddhist families often visit **temples** or **monasteries** to take part in **puja**, **meditation** or listen to **sacred texts**. In some countries, **monasteries** provide education to children and children receive schooling from **monks**.
Ceremonies to introduce children to the faith	Children become part of the faith at **baptism**, and this develops as they attend **church** and prepare for **confirmation** (see p.15).	After a baby is born, some Buddhists visit a **temple** and place the baby in front of a **shrine**. They provide **offerings** to the shrine to **give thanks** for the birth. In other Buddhist traditions, monks visit the **home** and give **blessings**.
Treatment of parents	Children are asked to **honour** their parents — to **look after** and **respect** them (Exodus 20:12).	Children are expected to treat their parents with **respect**. A child has duties to their parents which include doing as they ask and maintaining **family tradition**. "I will support them who supported me." *Sigalovada Sutta*

Families

Family life *in the UK has changed*

For a long time, the **nuclear family** was seen in Britain as the ideal family model. Religious families are **more likely** than the UK average to follow this model.
Today, it's common to find:

- **single-parent** families
- **unmarried** couples
- **reconstituted** (or **blended**) families
- **extended** families living together
- **same-sex** parents

nuclear family
A married man and woman, and their children

reconstituted (or **blended**) family
A couple and their children from previous relationships.

extended family
A family which includes grandparents, cousins etc.

1.8 children is the average...

Some people worry it's bad for children to grow up with same-sex parents, because they will only have **role models** from **one sex**.

Others argue that same-sex couples can provide a **stable**, **loving** home, which is what's important.

Extended families living together has become **more common** as people **live longer**, house prices **rise** and both parents **work**.

- Parents and children might **share** a home with grandparents to **save** money on housing.
- The grandparents can be **looked after** by the parents but also **help** look after the children.

Christians *try to welcome different families*

Welcoming

- Whatever their opinions on divorce and homosexuality, many Christians focus on making sure reconstituted families and single or same-sex parents feel **welcome** in church.
- It is **important** that families remain **connected** to the church, particularly so that any **children** will still be brought up in a **Christian way**.

> "[Catholics should take] solicitous care to make sure that [divorcees] do not consider themselves as separated from the Church." *Pope John Paul II, Familiaris Consortio 84*

Less welcoming

- Some Christians' views on divorce and homosexuality make it **difficult** for them to **accept** certain types of family.
- The Catholic Church is more strongly **against** same-sex parenting than many other denominations. Catholics believe homosexuality is **wrong** and God created men and women to form a family.
- Divorced Catholics aren't allowed to take **communion** (see p.12), which could mean they feel **unwelcome** in church.

Buddhism *is not centred around a particular type of family*

- Most Buddhists' views on families reflect the **culture** and **traditions** of the country they live in.
- Buddhists often live in **extended families** with grandparents and uncles and aunts all living in the **same house**. This is because parents and children have a duty to **respect** and **look after** each other (Sigalovada Sutta).
- Some Buddhists may not be **welcoming** to families made up of **same-sex couples** or **single parents**. This would most likely reflect the **culture** of the country the Buddhist lived in, e.g. a Buddhist living in Sri Lanka (where same-sex marriage is **illegal**) may be more likely to be **unwelcoming** to a family with a **same-sex couple** than a Buddhist in the **UK**.

EXAM QUESTION

It's never simple, is it...

Have a quick go at this exam question, just for a fun break...
Give two religious attitudes towards reconstituted families.

[2]

Gender Equality

Discrimination based on gender is widespread

Gender discrimination is a problem in British society, although the situation's **gradually improving**.

- **Gender stereotypes** (e.g. **women** being more **emotional** and **men** being more **confident**, or **fixed roles** for men and women) are now seen by many people as **false, unnecessary** and **damaging** to both genders.
- Some people argue there is still a **long way to go** before women are treated equally to men, e.g. as **well below half** of MPs are women. Others think the genders are now treated **equally**. A **minority** of people argue that it's now men who have it **worse**, e.g. because women are now more likely to go to university.

Men and women often have different roles in the home

Having different roles doesn't necessarily mean either are **unequal**,
but these **fixed ideas** make it **hard** for **either** gender to do the **opposite role**.

WOMEN
- **Taking care** of the **family** and **home** is often seen as the woman's role.
- Entitled to **52 weeks' maternity leave**, with **39 weeks** paid.
  - This is more than men, to reflect the fact that women **give birth** and many women **breastfeed**.
- Women often encounter **problems** in the **workplace** after taking time off to have children — many find their male colleagues have been **promoted** in the meantime, or struggle to afford **childcare** which would allow them to return to work.
- Women often still do **more housework** than men, even if they're working.

MEN
- The man's role has traditionally been to **earn money** to **support** the family.
  - This means that many men **don't** get to **look after** and **spend time** with their **children**.
- If the parents don't choose to take shared parental leave, men are only entitled to **2 weeks'** paid **paternity leave**. Some feel 2 weeks is **too little**.

Shared parental leave (SPL), introduced in the UK in **2015**, gives parents the option to **share** the time off work to look after their child in its first year. SPL involves the mother **giving up** part of her maternity leave so that the father can spend that time with the child instead. **Very few** fathers have taken SPL so far.

There are problems with equality in the workplace

Contrary to what many people believe, women have **always worked**.

In the past...
- Women were **prevented** from doing many jobs, by **law** or by **other people**.
- Some had to stop work when they **married**.
- Women were often **paid less** than men for the **same job**, or offered jobs with **less responsibility** and **lower pay**.

These **three** pieces of **legislation** have helped to **reduce** gender inequalities in the workplace:

1 Equal Pay Act 1970

2 Sex Discrimination Act 1975

These made gender discrimination **illegal**, e.g. by saying **both genders** had to be **paid** the **same amount** and have the **same working conditions** for the **same job**.

3 Equality Act 2010
This brought all the legislation together in **one act**. It also made **positive action** legal. The Act allows for '**occupational requirements**'.

positive action
action to help a group that's underrepresented in a profession or organisation. E.g. if a male-dominated company has two equally-qualified candidates for a job, it's legal for them to pick the female candidate to help women become better represented in the company.

occupational requirements
objective reasons why a certain group is best for a job. This means it's legal to, for example, only offer a male role in a play to male actors.

Despite these laws, some **problems remain**.

Today...
- There are professions in which **one gender** is **underrepresented**. **Nursing** or **midwifery** are seen as **women's** jobs, while **building** or **firefighting** are seen as **men's**.
- Women are **underrepresented** in **positions of authority**, e.g. as politicians or company directors.
- Many women still face **discrimination** at work, such as receiving **lower pay**, not being considered for **promotion** or being **sexually harassed**, although it's **illegal**.

It can be hard to prove discrimination happened. E.g. it's hard to tell if you're being paid less than someone else in the same job.

Gender Equality

Traditional gender roles were, and often still are, **supported** by **Christianity** and **Buddhism**.

The Bible is a bit unclear on the status of women

- The **Bible** gives messages both **against** and **in favour** of **gender discrimination**.

> "There is neither ... male [nor] female, for you are all one in Christ Jesus." *Galatians 3:28 NIV*

> "I do not permit a woman to teach or to assume authority over a man; she must be quiet." *1 Timothy 2:12 NIV*

- The Bible also says that wives should do as their husbands **tell them**:

> "Wives, submit ... to your own husbands as you do to the Lord. For the husband is the head of the wife as Christ is the head of the church..." *Ephesians 5:22-23 NIV*

- Many Christians say this reflects the **ideas** of **society** at the time, and doesn't correspond with **Jesus's attitude** towards women.
- Some of Jesus's followers were women, e.g. Mary and Martha (Luke 10:38-42), and he treated them **equally**.

Different denominations have different approaches to gender equality

Many Christians now believe men and women should be **equal**.

- The Catechism of the Catholic Church 1938 mentions *"sinful inequalities"* and says Catholics **fight against this**.
  - Despite this, the Catholic Church is still **more focused** on **traditional** gender roles than other denominations.

> "society should create and develop conditions favouring work in the home [for women]" *Pope John Paul II, Familiaris Consortio 23*

- For most of Christian history, women weren't allowed to be **priests**. This is no longer the case — women can now be **ministers** in most **Protestant** denominations, and **Anglican priests** and **bishops**. But they can't be **Roman Catholic** or **Orthodox** priests.

Buddhist views on familial gender roles are divided

- The Sigalovada Sutta provides **guidance** on the **different roles** of men and women within the family, but both roles are seen as **equally important**. Both men and women have a **duty** towards their families. Men are described as the **"providers"** for the family and women are expected to **run the household**.
- These roles reflect the **traditional roles** men and women played within their families in India during the time of the Buddha. Nowadays, Buddhists' views on gender roles tend to reflect the **culture** they live in. For example, many women in the UK are **providers** for their family, so a Buddhist in the UK is less likely to adhere to the gender roles described in the Sigalovada Sutta.

Buddhists have a range of views on gender equality

- The scriptures about women are **inconsistent**, so it's tricky to know what the Buddha thought.
- Some Buddhists follow the teaching in the Aparimitayur Sutra, which suggests a woman must be **reborn** as a man before **enlightenment** is possible.
- Other Buddhists follow the teachings of the Lotus Sutra, which says men and women are **equal**.

Buddhist men can become **monks** and women can become **nuns**, but this was not always the case. Buddha initially said women could not become nuns, but his **aunt** convinced him to change his mind. Allowing women to become nuns was quite **radical** at the time.

Some **Theravada** Buddhist monks see nuns as **subservient** to monks and some believe women should not be allowed to be **ordained** at all.

Hmmm... it's a tricky issue.

Learn specific examples to give in your answer, such as jobs where one gender is underrepresented.

Revision Summary

You might think you're done with this section... but I'm afraid there are a few **questions** for you to do first, just to see how much went in. These questions are like the questions you'll have in the **exam**, so you can **get used to** what you're meant to do and how much you should write.

If you're **not sure** about any of the answers, have another read of the section and then **try again**. **Tick off** each question when you get it right. For the last question there are **extra marks** available for your **spelling**, **punctuation** and **grammar**, so make sure your writing is accurate and that you check through it when you're done.

Let's start you off gently with 1 mark multiple choice questions.

1) Which of the following means preventing pregnancy?
    a) Conception   b) Cohabitation   c) Contraception   d) Conscience

2) Which of the following describes when an unmarried couple live together?
    a) Sex outside of marriage   b) Cohabitation   c) Heterosexuality   d) Promiscuity

3) Which of the following is the term for being married to more than one person?
    a) Procreation   b) Adultery   c) Arranged marriage   d) Polygamy

4) Which of the following is the phrase for the traditional view of men and women's roles?
    a) Gender discrimination   b) Same and equal   c) Separate but equal   d) Gender stereotypes

These questions are worth 2 marks, so you need to write down two brief points.

5) Give two religious beliefs about sexual relationships.

6) Give two religious beliefs about homosexuality.

7) Give two religious beliefs about the significance of procreation.

8) Give two religious beliefs about women's roles.

If you want top marks, you'll need to make sure your answers are well-developed for these questions — **they're worth 4 marks. Make sure your writing is well-organised and accurate so your points are clear.**

9) Explain two contrasting beliefs in British society today about promiscuity.

10) Explain two contrasting beliefs in British society today about the nuclear family model.

11) Explain two similar religious beliefs about women in work.

For this question, you must refer to the main religious tradition in the UK and Buddhism. **This question is worth 4 marks.**

12) Explain two contrasting religious beliefs about sex outside of marriage.

And add 1 more — these are worth 5 marks. You should refer to religious teachings or sacred texts.

13) Explain two religious beliefs about same-sex marriage.

14) Explain two religious beliefs about divorce.

15) Explain two religious beliefs about children's responsibilities towards their parents.

16) Explain two religious beliefs about non-traditional families.

This is the big one you've been waiting for — it's worth 12 marks and another 3 for SPaG. **You'll always be given a list like the one below of things you have to include.** **Use it to plan and structure your answer before you start the essay.** **It's worth noting down a list of arguments for and against so you're clear on what you need to write about.**

17) 'Marriage is a lifelong union between one man and one woman.'
    Evaluate this statement.
    Your answer should include the following:
    • religious arguments that support the statement
    • religious arguments that disagree with the statement
    • a conclusion
    You can also include non-religious points of view in your answer.

> Take a look at the 'Do Well in Your Exam' section — it gives advice on writing essays.

Theme A — Relationships and Families

The Origins of the Universe

No one saw exactly how the **Earth** came to be like it is... but science and religion both have their **theories**.

Scientific arguments — there are *two* **main types**

 1 **Cosmological theories** — how the Universe began

Chief amongst these is the **Big Bang** theory. It says that the Universe began in an **explosion** of matter and energy. Matter from this explosion eventually formed stars, planets and **everything** else. The Universe still seems to be expanding — important **evidence** for this theory.

 2 **Evolutionary theories** — how living things changed

Charles Darwin argued that life on Earth originated from simple cells. Life **evolved** (gradually changed) over millions of years into a huge variety of forms, and those **best adapted survived** — 'survival of the fittest'. According to this theory, people evolved from **apes**, not Adam and Eve.

Non-religious people look to **science** for answers. They believe that the universe and human life came about by **chance**. They say that since people evolved from **apes**, they can't have been created by God.

Religions *have their own ideas* about all this...

 Some religious people believe **only** in the stories written in **scriptures**.

 Others believe that **science** tells them **how** the world was created, but **religion** explains **why**. They believe that God **caused** the Big Bang, and evolution is the way he made humans.

 Genesis chapter 1 says God created everything over **six days**. On the seventh day he **rested**. Genesis chapters 1 and 2 describe how God created **people** in **his image**, and made **woman** from **man** (see p.5).

Some Christians believe the Bible gives a **literal** account of what happened. People who disagree with evolution claim there's a lack of proof backing up the theory — **fossils** don't show the **full process** of evolution.

Lots of Christians view the creation story as **symbolic** and also believe in scientific theories.

The Big Bang theory was actually first put forward by a Roman Catholic priest, Georges Lemaître, so religion and science don't have to be completely separate.

"Collaboration between religion and science is mutually beneficial..."
General Synod of the Church of England, 2010

Many Christians believe that science and religious ideas can exist in **harmony**. Both the Church of England and the Roman Catholic Church have recognised the **benefits** of the two working together.

"Evolution in nature does not conflict with the notion of Creation..."
Pope Francis, Pontifical Academy of Sciences, October 27 2014

 Some Buddhists believe that thinking about the origin of the universe is a **waste of time**. We will **never know** the answers to questions about the origin of the universe (we will die before we know them), so instead we should focus on finding **enlightenment**.

This is illustrated in the **Parable of the Poisoned Arrow** (Majjhima Nikaya, Sutta Pitaka), which tells the story of a man who is more preoccupied with finding out **who** shot him than he is with taking the arrow out of his body — because of this, he eventually **dies**.

In the **Agganna Sutta** (part of the Sutta Pitaka), the Buddha tells two men about the **beginning** of the **universe**. The description has many similarities with **scientific theories** about evolution, e.g. living creatures change gradually over time. In the Buddha's story, living things begin as **spirits** and slowly come to Earth due to **greed** and **desire** for things on Earth — like food and water.

Buddhists view the universe as **cyclical** (no beginning or end). This is reflected in the cyclical nature of **human existence** (**samsara**) and the cyclical nature of the **seasons** and other natural processes. This relates to **dependent arising** (see p.25), where everything is caused by something else.

 REVISION TASK

No monkeying around now — there's a lot to learn here...

Jot down as many beliefs about the origin of the universe as you can for each religion.

General	# The Environment and Stewardship

Religious believers think people should look after the environment because it was created by God.

The world is a way for God to reveal his presence

Many believers appreciate the world and what's in it because it is God's creation. They feel that he reveals himself constantly in the world through experiences that inspire awe and wonder, where someone can feel God's presence.

But people don't always take good care of the world we live in...

> For example, a beautiful sunset, a wild sea or a butterfly's wing might convince someone there must be a creator.

Humans have damaged the environment

Global Warming

- Gases in the atmosphere, called 'greenhouse gases', help keep the Earth warm.
- Over the past century, the amount of greenhouse gas in the atmosphere has increased, and measurements show that the Earth has got hotter. This is called global warming. Higher temperatures have an effect on global weather patterns and make ice melt, which causes sea levels to rise. This could lead to flooding in low-lying areas.
- It is mainly caused by the fuels used to generate energy, like oil, coal and gas.

Natural Resources

A natural resource is anything found naturally that's useful to humans.

- The Earth's population is increasing and people use more raw materials and more energy every year. If people carry on like this, many natural resources will eventually run out.
- Fertile land for growing crops is also rapidly declining. Each year, overgrazing and irresponsible farming methods turn more fertile land into desert.

Pollution

Pollution from chemicals can contaminate the environment.

- Sewage and chemicals can pollute lakes, rivers and seas. These pollutants harm the plants and animals that live in and around the water, including humans.
- People use toxic chemicals for farming. They also bury nuclear waste underground, and dump a lot of household and industrial waste in landfill sites. The toxic chemicals can kill plants and animals, and cause cancer in humans.
- Smoke and gases from vehicles and industry can pollute the air, cause health problems in humans and damage the ozone layer.

The Environment and Stewardship

There are many ways to tackle environmental problems

Many people, both religious and non-religious, work to **reduce** and **repair** the harm caused to the **environment**. They think that it's important to look after the planet for **future generations**.

> There's a **limit** to the Earth's resources, so many people believe it's important to be able to **manage** the resources currently available and to find alternative, **sustainable** options too.

> Lots of people try to be environmentally friendly by **recycling** things like paper and plastic.

> They may also take **public transport** or **walk** to cut down on pollution caused by vehicle fumes and to use less fuel.

> Some also **campaign** to better inform others about the damage being done to the environment and how to live more sustainably.

Christians and Buddhists believe in looking after the environment

Many religious believers feel it's their **duty** to look after the environment.

CHRISTIANITY	BUDDHISM
• God spoke of humanity's power over nature: **"...rule over the fish in the sea and the birds in the sky, over the livestock and all the wild animals..."** *Genesis 1:26 NIV* This power is known as **dominion**. Some people think it means humans can use the environment **however** they want. • God made Christians **stewards** of the **environment**: **"The Lord God took the man and put him in the Garden of Eden to work it and take care of it."** *Genesis 2:15 NIV* • Christians have no right to **abuse** God's creation, and they have a **responsibility** to protect it: **"humanity's dominion cannot be understood as licence to abuse, spoil, squander or destroy what God has made..."** *Christian Declaration on Nature, Assisi 1986* • Everything is **interdependent** (everything depends on everything else), so driving species of animal or plant to **extinction**, or harming the planet, eventually ends up harming people. • The damage humans do to the environment **clashes** with their role as stewards. Christian organisations such as **CAFOD**, **Christian Aid** and **Tearfund**® are concerned with putting this responsibility into practice. They put pressure on **governments** and **industry** to think more about how people are abusing the planet.	• Many Buddhists believe they should look after the environment because of **dependent arising**. Everything is **interconnected** and humans rely on the environment for many aspects of life, e.g. oxygen. • One part of the **Eightfold Path** (see p.30) is having the **right livelihood**. For many Buddhists, this would include having a job that does not have **negative effects** on the environment, e.g. not working for a company that destroys forests. Some Buddhists believe that working in a job like this would produce **negative karma**. • Many Buddhists want to look after the environment in order to **avoid suffering**, e.g. destroying the natural habitats of animals leads to **great suffering** and even **death** for the animals who live there. • In the Dhammapada (a collection of Buddha's sayings), there is a description of a **bee** that does not cause any harm to the environment. Some Buddhists take this to mean that **humans** should go about their work in the **same way**. **"As a bee gathers honey from the flower without injuring its colour or fragrance."** *Dhammapada 49*

Look after the environment — it's the natural thing to do...

Define stewardship, then write a few points about how people might carry it out.

Christianity & Buddhism

Animal Rights

You need to know about **views** on animal experimentation in **Christianity** and **one other religious tradition**.

Animal experimentation *and* vegetarianism *are key issues*

Animals are sometimes used... **...to test products** used by humans or for **medical experiments**

- Some people see this as **cruel**.
- Others look at the issue in a **utilitarian** way. They argue that animal testing is **acceptable** if it could help many people, even if animals suffer.

...for food
- Some say that humans are **built** to **consume meat**.
- Other people argue that hurting animals is wrong, so it's better to be **vegetarian** or **vegan**.

> **utilitarianism**
> *the idea that decisions should be made based on what has the best balance of good and bad outcomes*

Christians *have different beliefs on how animals should be* treated ✝

Due to **different interpretations** of the Bible, there isn't just one Christian belief about animal rights:

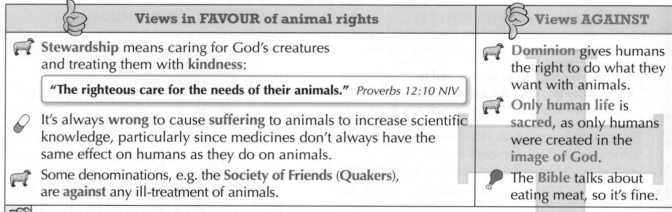

👍 Views in FAVOUR of animal rights	👎 Views AGAINST
🐑 **Stewardship** means caring for God's creatures and treating them with **kindness**: *"The righteous care for the needs of their animals."* Proverbs 12:10 NIV It's always **wrong** to cause **suffering** to animals to increase scientific knowledge, particularly since medicines don't always have the same effect on humans as they do on animals. 🐑 Some denominations, e.g. the **Society of Friends** (**Quakers**), are **against** any ill-treatment of animals.	🐑 **Dominion** gives humans the right to do what they want with animals. 🐑 **Only human life** is **sacred**, as only humans were created in the **image of God**. 🍗 The **Bible** talks about eating meat, so it's fine.

MIXED views

Animal testing is tolerated only if it benefits mankind, and the animals' suffering is considered:

> **"Medical and scientific experimentation on animals is a morally acceptable practice if it remains within reasonable limits and contributes to caring for or saving human lives. It is contrary to human dignity to cause animals to suffer or die needlessly."** *Catechism of the Catholic Church, 2417-2418*

Christianity has no specific food laws so **vegetarianism** (not eating meat) and **veganism** (not eating or using any animal products) are matters for **individuals** to decide about.

Buddhism *teaches people not to harm* living things

- Most Buddhists show **compassion** (see p.33) for animals and try to avoid **unnecessary suffering**, e.g. they may think animal suffering is only acceptable if there is the **right intention**, such as feeding a family.
- The **first Moral Precept** (see p.34) instructs Buddhists **not to kill**. Many Buddhists believe this includes animals and so choose to be **vegetarians** and only buy **products** that have not been **tested on animals**.

> Animals are part of the cycle of **samsara** — some Buddhists believe you can be **reborn** as an **animal**. Being reborn as an animal is not desirable because animals cannot make **conscious choices** — this means there is no opportunity to extinguish the **Three Poisons** and find **enlightenment**. For this reason, some Buddhists may choose to **eat meat** or support **animal testing** of medicines.

Animal rights shouldn't be left out...

Summarise what each religion teaches about animal rights. Try to mention sacred texts too.

Abortion and Euthanasia

Make sure you know the views of **non-religious** people, **Christians** and **Buddhists** on abortion and euthanasia.

Abortion and euthanasia are legal under certain conditions

There are different **types** of euthanasia and different **laws** in the UK for abortion and euthanasia. The **table** below tells you all you need to know about this:

Term	Definition	Treatment by UK law
abortion	*when a foetus is removed prematurely from the womb before it can survive*	**Legal** in the UK and can take place until the **24th week** of pregnancy. Abortions can take place **after** this time if there's a **danger** to the **health** of the mother or foetus.
euthanasia	*killing someone to relieve suffering (often from an incurable disease)*	**Varies** depending on if the euthanasia is **passive** or **active**.
active euthanasia	*helping someone who wants to end their own suffering to die*	**Illegal** in the UK, but legal in some countries, e.g. **Belgium**.
passive euthanasia	*withdrawing medical treatment that might extend someone's life*	**Legal** in the UK.

Abortion and euthanasia are controversial issues

Many atheists support abortion as it gives women **control** over what happens to their **bodies**. Humanists **prioritise** quality of life over sustaining life, and look at the **impact** on the **woman** first.

HOWEVER... there is some **debate** surrounding the **time limit** on abortions:

 Since some babies born **prematurely** at 24 weeks or less **survive**, some feel that the **timeframe** for abortions should be **shortened**.

 Others feel that there **shouldn't** be a time limit on abortions at all.

There is even more of a **divide** in opinions when it comes to **euthanasia**:

 Some support it when a person will **die** from an illness or where they are suffering from an **incurable** illness. They feel that ending someone's **suffering** through euthanasia is the **kindest** thing to do.

 However, some people fear that **legalising** euthanasia would potentially lead to people feeling **pressured** into it. Some also feel that **doctors** should work to **protect** lives, not the opposite.

With abortion and euthanasia, many people look at the factors of each particular case — this is known as **situation ethics**. They think **decisions** should be made based on what is best in **each situation**, not by following **rules** that should apply to **every instance**.

Christianity | Abortion and Euthanasia

Christians are generally *against* abortion and euthanasia

| All life is created by God. | → | As God's creation, all life belongs to God and is therefore holy. | → | This is the 'sanctity of life' argument. |

Based on this 'sanctity of life' argument, many religious people believe that people don't have the right to interfere with when life ends, or to prevent new life. Other people take into consideration a person's quality of life (how able they are to live a normal life).

Christian views AGAINST...	MIXED views on...

...abortion
 	
• Abortion is undesirable as God *"created mankind in his own image"* (Genesis 1:27 NIV).
  • The Roman Catholic Church goes so far as to say that abortion is murder, as it teaches that human life starts as soon as the egg is fertilised at conception.
 	
  "...all direct abortion... [is] to be absolutely excluded as lawful means of regulating the number of children." Humanae Vitae, section 14
 	
• Abortion is wrong because God cares about all of His children.
 	
• Some Christian writings (e.g. the Didache, a 2nd century manual of Christian teaching) are quite specifically against abortion.
	• Abortion is permissible in certain circumstances, such as when the pregnancy puts the mother's life at risk. The life of the unborn child cannot be valued above the mother.
	
	• Allowing a woman to choose is a way of showing Christian compassion — regardless of whether or not they agree with the woman's choice or not.
	
	• The Bible doesn't actually mention abortion, but it connects life with breath, e.g. in the creation of Adam — so it could be argued that the foetus is only alive when it breathes.

...euthanasia
 	
• Roman Catholics believe that anything that intentionally causes death is wrong. So even those who are unlikely to recover should be kept alive.
 	
  "...an act or omission which... causes death in order to eliminate suffering constitutes a murder..." Catechism of the Catholic Church, 2277
 	
• Euthanasia goes against the commandment *"You shall not murder"*. Only God should decide when a person's life ends, as he initially gave them life.
 	
• Suffering is part of life. Job was made to suffer by Satan, but refused to end his life:
 	
  "Shall we accept good from God, and not trouble?" Job 2:10 NIV
 	
• Euthanasia could be seen to ruin the natural course of death, when a soul starts to make its way to God.
 	
• Many Christians feel they must care for sick people, and euthanasia goes against this. Local churches often have links with hospices — a hospice is a place where terminally ill people can be well cared for. This allows a person to feel valued as they reach the end of their life.
	• The use of 'extraordinary treatment' (e.g. life-support machines which are keeping someone alive artificially) is not always the best approach — the easing of suffering through passive euthanasia is a way of demonstrating Christian compassion.
	  • However, many only agree with euthanasia if the dying person chooses it for themselves.

	• Anglican denominations are against active euthanasia. However, they agree that terrible distress should not be suffered at all costs, and that death may be considered a blessing rather than continuing life-extending treatment. They argue that a person's quality of life must also be considered.

Abortion and Euthanasia 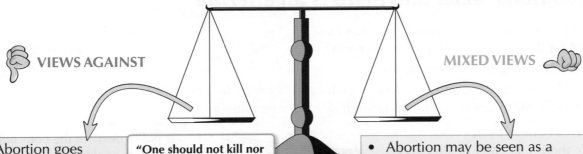 Buddhism

Buddhists have differing views on abortion

👎 VIEWS AGAINST   MIXED VIEWS 🤏

"One should not kill nor cause another to kill."
Dhammapada 130

- Abortion goes against the **first** of the **Five Moral Precepts** — do not **kill** or **harm** a **living thing**.
- Abortion provides **bad karma** for the **mother** (due to breaking the First Moral Precept) and also for the **unborn foetus**, as the foetus doesn't get the opportunity to find **enlightenment**.
- Having the **intention** to kill is seen as a **wrong intention** for many Buddhists, which goes against the **Eightfold Path**.

- Abortion may be seen as a **compassionate** thing to do in **some circumstances**, e.g. if **medical conditions** mean the child will live with **suffering**.
- Some Buddhists believe that if the woman has a **right intention** then abortion can be permissible, e.g. if the intention is to save the **mother's life**, not kill the child.
- In **Japan**, abortion is very common and some Japanese Buddhists take part in **Mizuko Kuyo** — a special ceremony for aborted and miscarried babies.

Many Buddhists are against euthanasia

- Euthanasia also goes against the **first** of the **Five Moral Precepts** — do not **kill** or **harm** a **living thing**.
- Some Buddhists think that **suffering** is a result of **bad karma** from a **previous life** and so the suffering must be **endured**. Euthanasia will only **delay** the suffering into your **next life**.
- **Hospices** are a far better way to reduce suffering for the terminally ill and give them a **good death** (calm and peaceful).

HOWEVER... some Buddhists **support** euthanasia in **certain circumstances**:

 Many Buddhists believe that having a **good death** is important. This involves trying to **reduce suffering** and help **calm** the dying person. Euthanasia would allow someone who is in a lot of pain to **suffer less**.

 Euthanasia may be the most **compassionate** thing to do for someone if they are **suffering**.

 If the **intention** of euthanasia is to **reduce suffering**, rather than to kill, then some Buddhists may see it as **acceptable**.

 EXAM TIP
The last few pages have covered a lot of information
...so go back over them if you need to. You need to be able to talk about views on abortion and euthanasia in Christianity and Buddhism, so make sure you know the differences between them.

The Afterlife

Every religion in the world has something to say about **death** — and what comes **after** it.

Most religions teach that there is an afterlife

- Some religions teach that the soul is **rewarded** or **punished** for the **actions** of the person on Earth.
- Others believe the soul is **reincarnated**.
- Christians believe that life on Earth isn't **everything** — a **better life** awaits them. It's still **important** though, and is **preparation** for the afterlife.

> **afterlife** (life after death)
> *a different kind of existence for the soul after the body has died*

CHRISTIANS believe Jesus's **resurrection** shows that there's life after death.

Christianity teaches that people go to **heaven** or **hell**, depending on how God **judges** their actions — trying to live life according to Christian **teachings** and believing in **Jesus** will allow them to receive **God's grace** and go to **heaven**.

Catholics believe that some go to **Purgatory** — a place where **sins** are **paid for** before going to heaven (see p.8).

> *"He was put to death in the body but made alive in the Spirit."* 1 Peter 3:18 NIV

> *"And God raised us up with Christ and seated us with him in the heavenly realms in Christ Jesus... For it is by grace you have been saved..."* Ephesians 2:6-8 NIV

> *"long is worldly existence to fools who know not the Sublime Truth"* Dhammapada 60

BUDDHISTS do not believe in an afterlife where the self or soul will continue. This is because they believe there is **no fixed self** (anatta).

Instead, Buddhists believe in **rebirth**, where a person's **energy** continues in a **new life**. The cycle of rebirth is called **samsara** and it will not end until a person finds **enlightenment** and reaches **nibbana**.

Some Buddhists believe that after a person reaches nibbana, they will **no longer be reborn**.	**Mahayana Buddhists** think that you can choose to become a **Bodhisattva** and stay on Earth to help others find **enlightenment**.	**Pure Land Buddhists** believe they will be reborn into a **paradise world** or 'Pure Land' called Sukhavati where they can continue their journey to find **enlightenment**.

Many **NON-RELIGIOUS** people believe that when you die, that's it — you **cease to exist**. There isn't any **concrete evidence** that there is life after death, so the **logical** answer is that it **doesn't exist**:

'Believing in an afterlife is just a way of **helping** people deal with **death** — the idea gives **comfort**.'

'The idea of an afterlife is used by religions to put **pressure** on people to **follow** their teachings and **live** their lives in a certain way.'

There are many **arguments** used by both **religious** and **non-religious** people to **support** life after death:

 The **paranormal** (things science can't explain, which are thought to have a spiritual cause, e.g. **ghosts**) is sometimes used as evidence. Some people (**mediums**) claim they can **talk** to the **dead**.

 Some people claim to have evidence of **reincarnation** (they lived a previous life, died, and were reborn in a new body). Lots of research has been carried out with young **children** who claim to remember **past lives**.

 People say they've had a **near-death** or **out-of-body experience** where they've spoken to long-dead **family members**.

 Some believe there must be **more** after **life on Earth**. They might see going to heaven or paradise as a **reward** for people who've been **good** all their lives — it must exist to **compensate** for the **unfairness** of life on Earth.

 It might not seem like it now, but there is life after exams...
Explain two reasons religious people believe in life after death. Use sacred text references. [5]

Revision Summary

Those were some pretty big issues that you've just read about — now let's see how much you can **remember**. These questions will let you get a feel for how the **exam** will be, and how **much writing** is involved.

If there's anything you can't answer, **go back** through the section and have another go when you've **re-read** it. For the last question there are **extra marks** for **spelling**, **punctuation** and **grammar**, so check your writing carefully.

Getting the ball rolling with some 1 mark questions — they're even multiple choice.

1) Which of the following is the theory that humans evolved from apes?
   a) The Big Bang   b) Reincarnation   c) Evolution   d) Dependent Arising

2) Which of the following is the idea that believers must look after God's creation?
   a) Veganism   b) Dominion   c) Stewardship   d) Samsara

3) Which of the following words means to terminate a pregnancy?
   a) Abortion   b) Euthanasia   c) Conception   d) Purgatory

4) Which of the following is the approach of making decisions by looking at each individual case?
   a) Utilitarianism   b) Situation ethics   c) Humanism   d) Compassion

Let's make things a little trickier. 2 marks = 2 short points.

5) Give two religious beliefs about how people might experience God's presence through the natural world.

6) Give two examples of what religious people could do to protect the environment.

7) Give two religious beliefs about dominion.

8) Give two religious beliefs about eating meat.

Moving up to 4 marks. Make two points, but this time develop them further to get an extra mark for each. Talk about the views of one or both religions.

Make sure that you write clearly and organise your answer well for the longer answer questions.

9) Explain two different religious beliefs about how the human race began.

10) Explain two similar religious beliefs about the value of life.

11) Explain two similar religious beliefs about what happens after death.

For this question, you must refer to the main religious tradition in the UK and at least one other religious viewpoint. There are 4 marks available for this question.

12) Explain two contrasting beliefs about animal experimentation in Britain today.

5 marks up for grabs now. You'll need to refer to religious texts for top marks.

13) Explain two religious beliefs about how the world was created.

14) Explain two religious beliefs about evolution.

15) Explain two religious beliefs about stewardship.

16) Explain two religious beliefs about abortion.

And last but not least — the 12 mark question (with another 3 marks for SPaG). The question will always come with bullet points that you should include in your answer, so use them to make a plan before you begin. Think about arguments in favour of and against the statement, and pack your answer full of information.

17) 'Euthanasia can be the most compassionate way to help someone who is terminally ill.'
    Evaluate this statement.
    Your answer should include the following:
    • religious arguments that support the statement
    • religious arguments that disagree with the statement
    • a conclusion
    You can also include non-religious points of view in your answer.

Turn to the 'Do Well in Your Exam' section for more about writing essays.

Theme B — Religion and Life

Design and Causation

The belief that God **created** the world is an **important part** of **many religions**, and often strengthens **faith**.

Different people *believe for different reasons*

- About **84%** of the global population belongs to a religion (source: Pew Research Center).
- The rest don't have specific religious beliefs, or have **no spiritual beliefs**.

There are **various reasons** why people might **FOLLOW** or **REJECT** religion:

FOLLOW
- People want to find out **why** life is as it is. Some people are convinced the 'design' or 'causation' arguments explain this.
- Some are drawn to the **purpose**, **structure** and **comfort** religion provides, or simply by the desire to have something to **believe**.
- Some people's faith is strengthened by the feelings they experience during **worship** and as part of a religious **community**.
- People brought up by religious **parents** or in a religious **community** are more likely to believe in a god.

REJECT
- There's **no proof** there's a **god**.
- Religion causes too much **strife** between people.
- The **evil** in the world shows there's no god.

- **Atheists reject** the idea of a **divine being**.
- **Agnostics** believe it's **impossible** to know **either way** for **certain**.

The design argument: 'The Universe *must have had a designer*'

- Belief that God **created** the universe is a **central** part of **belief in God** — not only does the Universe's existence **prove** God's existence, but believers think it shows some of his **characteristics**, e.g. his **power**.

- Many Christians believe a god **exists** because of 'design' arguments. The idea is that the **intricate workings** of the **universe** can't have come about by **chance**. There must have been some kind of **designer** — a god. The Bible **support** this argument.

"...since the creation of the world God's invisible qualities — his eternal power and divine nature — have been clearly seen, being understood from what has been made." Romans 1:20 NIV

- Some think aspects of **nature** support this idea. E.g., **snowflakes** form **complex** shapes that are **unique** to each **individual** snowflake.

 William Paley's **watchmaker argument** says that if you came across an intricate **watch**, you wouldn't think it was made **by chance** — you would assume it had been **designed**. The same must be true of **complex structures** in **nature**.

- **Scientists** say the **conditions** that led to the **creation** of the **universe** and **life** were extremely **specific**. The **fine-tuning argument** says this shows there was a **designer** — they couldn't have occurred by **chance**.

Some people *aren't convinced by these arguments*

- In **2009**, a survey found **37%** of people in **Britain** thought **evolution** was 'beyond reasonable doubt'.

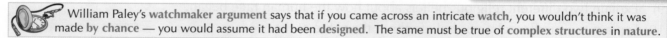 **Charles Darwin** explained how species **developed** by **adapting** themselves to the **conditions** around them through '**survival of the fittest**'. **Species** or **individuals** that have **characteristics** that are **beneficial** for **survival** are **more likely** to live, while those that **aren't** well-adapted are **more likely** to **die out**. This helps to explain how species have **developed** their **characteristics** through **time** — known as **evolution**.

Darwin didn't see evolution as conclusive proof against God's existence.

- **Buddhists** do not believe that the universe was created by a god. Many Buddhists **accept scientific theories** about the origins of the universe because they do not conflict with Buddhism. Buddhism is concerned with **alleviating suffering** and finding **enlightenment** in life — questions about the origins of the universe are not relevant to this.

The current **Dalai Lama** (leader of Tibetan Buddhism) is passionate about science and wrote a book called "**The Universe in a Single Atom**", which encourages Buddhists to accept **scientific theories** about the origins of the universe.

- Followers of **Christianity** have differing views on evolution:

 Evolution **doesn't** contradict the **design argument** — God must have 'designed' evolution. **vs.** It's a struggle to **reconcile** evolution with the belief that God created **humans** in his own **image** — it seems **unlikely** he would have done so by **slowly evolving** humans from apes.

- **Non-religious** people may also hold a range of views, for example:

 God **created** the universe but has not had any **further involvement** with it. **vs.** There's **no evidence** the 'designer' and creator still exists.

Design and Causation

Ideas about **causation** have been used over the **centuries** as evidence that a divine being **exists**.

Causation: 'There must have been a *first cause*'

The **First Cause** argument, also known as the **cosmological argument**, is founded on a **chain of logic**. Everything that **happens** is **caused** by **something else**. An event **now** was caused by an **earlier** event, that was caused by an **even earlier** event, etc. If you trace this **chain** back in time, there are **two** possibilities:

1 The chain goes back **forever** — i.e. the universe has **always** existed, it's **eternal**.

2 You eventually reach a **starting point** — an **uncaused** cause or '**First Cause**'.

Some think the '**First Cause**' was **God**, as only he is **eternal** and has enough **power** to create the universe.

Religious figures *have* theorised *about the First Cause*

Buddhism

Buddhists **do not believe** that an omnipotent god created the universe. They view the universe as **cyclical** — with **no beginning or end**.

In '**The Universe in a Single Atom**' the 14th Dalai Lama says that neither **Buddhism nor science** require the belief in a god as a **Creator**.

Christianity

Thomas Aquinas, a 13th century monk, developed Five Ways to prove God exists. They've been influential in Christianity. Three of them have a similar logic to the 'First Cause' theory:

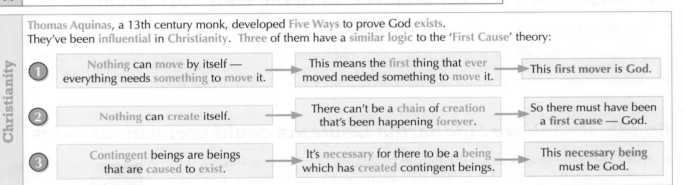

1 Nothing can **move** by itself — everything needs **something** to **move** it. → This means the first thing that ever moved needed something to move it. → This **first mover is God**.

2 **Nothing** can **create** itself. → There can't be a **chain** of **creation** that's been happening **forever**. → So there must have been a **first cause** — God.

3 **Contingent** beings are beings that are **caused** to **exist**. → It's **necessary** for there to be a being which has **created** contingent beings. → This **necessary being** must be God.

There are differing opinions *on the First Cause argument*

Many Christians use the First Cause argument as **evidence** there is a **god**, often in **combination** with **accounts** from the **scriptures** and the **design** argument. However, some people question its **logic**:

The argument **contradicts** itself — it says **everything** has to have a **cause**, but then says there must be an **event** that didn't have a **cause** — the **first cause**.

There's **no evidence** that if there is a **first cause**, it has to be a **divine being** — a god.

Even if a **god** was the **first cause**, it doesn't mean they **still** exist now. It also doesn't give any **indication** that the god has the **characteristics** of the **Christian god**.

Sacred texts *are used as* evidence *that God created the world*

✝ **Christian** teachings on **creation** are taken from Genesis 1, which says God created **everything**. The process took **6** days, and people **didn't evolve** from **apes**, but **descended** from **Adam** and **Eve**.

Some believers take the descriptions in the sacred texts **literally**, e.g. some Christians accept the account given in Genesis.

Others see the accounts as **symbolic** — they still believe God is the creator, but they look to science to explain how it all happened

Blimey, it's enough to make your head spin...

It's a good idea to read these two pages again to get them in your head — they're pretty complex.

Christianity & Buddhism

Miracles

As well as learning **both religions'** beliefs, make sure you can compare **Christian** and **non-religious** views.

Many believe *miracles prove* there is a God

- Christians believe in miracles, though to differing extents.
- These include events in their scriptures, though some people believe miracles also happen nowadays.
- Others argue that the miracles in religious texts should be interpreted symbolically rather than literally.
- Beliefs about miracles include:

> **miracles**
> *seemingly inexplicable events, such as people with apparently incurable illnesses being healed*

> They offer proof there is a god because they go against the laws of nature — only God would have the power to do so.

> They also show God's benevolence, as many miracles are beneficial, e.g. healing someone who is ill.

> Healing people also shows that God can decide who lives or dies.

Christians *read stories* of miracles *in the* New Testament

- Jesus performed miracles to show he had the power of God, and to show the importance of faith.

  > Examples include the feeding of the 5000 and healing a blind man — see p.93 for more detail.

- Christians believe the birth and resurrection of Jesus were miracles in their own right.

Buddhists *believe* Siddhartha Gautama *could perform* miracles

- There are many stories about the Buddha levitating, teleporting and performing healing miracles during his lifetime — e.g. he levitated over the Rohini River in order to stop a fight that was about to start over the water.

- Buddhists do not believe the Buddha is a god, but that he was able to perform miracles due to his enlightenment and through the power of meditation.
- Other enlightened beings, such as the Buddha's disciples, were also believed to have performed miracles through meditation.

Some people *don't believe* in miracles

- Some believers prefer to focus on God or living their life in a moral way, rather than on miracles.
- Atheists and humanists don't believe in miracles. They believe they can either be explained scientifically, or are fakes or misunderstandings.

  > For example, they might explain someone being cured of a terminal disease by saying they must have been misdiagnosed, or the hope of a religious figure healing them had stimulated their recovery — called the placebo effect, this also happens when people are given fake pills.

- It can be a matter of perspective — a religious person might seek a miraculous explanation for something atheists and humanists would call a coincidence, e.g. something happening soon after you prayed for it.

Don't rely on a miracle to pass your exam — revise well...

... and do exam questions. Miraculously, we've got one here:
Explain two contrasting beliefs about miracles.
Refer to the main religious tradition of Great Britain as well as non-religious beliefs.　　　[4]

Revelation

For **nature as revelation** and **visions**, you need to be able to compare **Christian** and **non-religious** views.

Revelation *is how God's presence is revealed*

- It's **difficult** to **conclusively prove** God **exists**. So Christians look for **evidence** to reveal God's **presence**. They believe he is **revealed** in **different** ways, including through the **scriptures**, the **world** around us and **religious experiences**.

- Revelation doesn't just involve knowing God **exists**, but also what he's **like** and what he **expects** of people. Revelations can **give rise to** or **strengthen** people's **belief** in a god.

- There are **two** main types of **revelation** — **special** revelation and **general** revelation:

Special Revelation	General Revelation
• **Special revelations** are revelations to **specific** people. • They include revelations through **prophethood** (written down as **scriptures**), **visions** and **miracles**. • They're **direct** and **personal**, so they can be **powerful** experiences. However, they're hard to **prove**. • Some think they **still** occur today, while others **disagree**.	• **General revelations** are revelations **available** to **everyone**. They're more **indirect** and therefore have to be **interpreted**. • Many think the **world** is an **example** of **general revelation**. **Believers** think God **created** the world, so it **proves** he exists. • Many think our **conscience** proves God exists, as people all over the world have **similar morals**, e.g. that **killing** is wrong. God must have **created** this within **every person**.

The *scriptures* are *important revelations for Christians*

- **Christians** believe God's **nature** and **will** are revealed in their **holy books**. Many believe they were either **inspired** by **God** or came **directly** from him. They contain **knowledge** of **God** and the **faith**.

- Most religious people believe that **all** or **parts** of them were **special revelations**, as they were revealed to **specific prophets**. In their **written** form, they also have some **features** of **general revelation** — they are **available** to **everyone**, all the **time**, and they need to be **interpreted** to be **understood**.

The Bible	
✝	• The Bible is a **collection** of books written by **various** authors. • Some Christians think the authors were **inspired** and **guided** by God as they **wrote**, but he didn't **directly** reveal it to them. • The **New Testament** describes Jesus's **life** — Jesus is seen as the **completion** of God's **revelation** to people. • **Jesus** is seen as the '**new covenant**' — he **died** for people's **sins**, but in return **people** should **worship** God.

> ✝ **"God spoke to our ancestors through the prophets at many times and in various ways, but in these last days he has spoken to us by his son"** *Hebrews 1:1-2 NIV*

- **Christians** believe revelations show God's **nature**. He is:

• **omniscient** — all-knowing • **infinite** — he has no limits • **omnipotent** — all-powerful • **transcendent** — beyond this world • **immanent** — involved in the world	• **eternal** — he has always existed and always will • the **creator** and **sustainer** of the universe — he made it and keeps it going • **all-loving** — infinite in his mercy and compassion and completely **good** • **personal** — believers can have a **relationship** with God, e.g. through **prayer** • **impersonal** — others see him as **distant** from people as he **rarely** acts in the world

- The scriptures can show God's **characteristics**. E.g. this verse suggests to believers that God is **personal**:

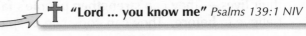

> ✝ **"Lord ... you know me"** *Psalms 139:1 NIV*

- Believers think God shows his **compassion** through his **intervention** in the world — e.g. showing people how to live a **better life** through the **prophets** and through **Jesus** as Messiah.

- Many **atheists** and **humanists** think the scriptures depict their authors' **ideas** about **God**, and that many of the events in them **didn't occur**. They may see these ancient texts as largely **irrelevant** to **life today**.

Buddhists *believe the Buddha* revealed the *truth about life*

- Buddhists **do not believe** in a god, so revelation has a **different meaning** in Buddhism.

- Buddhists believe that the **truth about life** was revealed by **the Buddha** through the **Four Noble Truths**. Buddhists follow the **Dhamma** and **meditate** in order to become **enlightened** and also have this truth revealed to them.

Revelation

Some see nature as revelation

- Christians believe **God** created the **world**, so it **shows** God **exists**.
- Many believers feel that nature provides **numinous** experiences. These are events that inspire **awe** and **wonder**, where someone can feel God's **presence**, e.g. a beautiful **sunset** might convince them there is a **creator**.

numinous
spiritual

- **Interventions** in **nature**, e.g. **miracles**, show God's **immanence**. Nature may show God's **transcendence** — he **created** it but isn't **present** in it — as well as other **aspects**:

 Characteristics such as God's **intelligence** are revealed through the **complexity** of nature. Nature is often **cruel**, which can be hard to explain. Some believe nature became **cruel** after the **Fall** — when Adam and Eve **sinned**. So nature no longer fully shows what God is **like**.

"The heavens declare the glory of God; the skies proclaim the work of his hands." *Psalms 19:1 NIV*

"The beauty of creation reflects the infinite beauty of the Creator." *Catechism of the Catholic Church 341*

 Buddhists do not believe the world was created by a god, but they do think the **natural world** is very important — humans rely on the world around them and all things are **interconnected**. Because of this, many Buddhists choose to spend a lot of time in the natural world, away from **distractions**. This is so they can extinguish the **Three Poisons** (see p.29) and **meditate**. E.g. Siddhartha Gautama found enlightenment when he was underneath the **Bodhi Tree**.

Atheists and **humanists** don't believe that **nature** reveals **God**. They argue that even aspects of **nature** we don't fully understand, e.g. how animals **navigate** as they **migrate**, will one day be **explained** by **science**.

God can be revealed through religious experiences

Religious experiences are **personal experiences** of God — they're a form of **special revelation**.

- They can take many **forms**, such as:
  - a vision
  - a dream
  - hearing a voice
  - a feeling of ecstasy or peace
  - feelings of being loved, forgiven or guided
- They can take place during **prayer** or **worship**, or at **other times**.
- They can be so **powerful** they **change** the **life** of the person, or they might be more gentle experiences.
- Other religious **believers** may take **inspiration** from someone who's had such an experience. Some people who have had religious experiences become **well known** — see below and the next page.

There are many examples of visions in Christianity

- A **vision** is a religious experience in which a person sees something **sacred** — such as an **angel**. **Visions** usually tell the receiver about **God** and his **will**, or about the receiver's **own life**.
- Visions are **direct** and **powerful** forms of religious experience. They often **change** how believers **live** their **lives** — they can **strengthen** people's **faith** or even **induce** them to believe in something they **didn't** believe in **before**. They can convince people that **God exists** — only **he** could have made them **happen**.
- Some **visions** are reported in the **Bible**, which gives them **authority**, as they're part of the **scripture**.

The **disciples** saw a vision of **Moses** and **Elijah** with Jesus, who was covered in **light** — see Matthew 17:1-13 and p.94.

St Paul was originally named **Saul**. He **persecuted** Christians. One day he saw a **light**, and heard **Jesus** asking **why** Saul was **persecuting** him. This **transformed** Saul's life — he became **Christian** and spent the rest of his life preaching the **gospel**.

- Other visions of **Mary** or **angels** appeared to people **later**. The Churches confirm if they think they're **authentic**. **Belief** in this type of vision is more **significant** in **Catholicism** than in **Protestant** Christianity.

Joan of Arc was a French peasant. She had **visions** of the **archangel Michael**, among others. These encouraged her to lead **France** against **England** in the **Hundred Years' War**. She was **captured** and **killed** by English allies. The **Catholic Church** declared her a **saint** — Catholics think her visions were **genuine**.

Many Catholics report visions of **Mary**. One example is **Bernadette Soubirous**, who claimed she saw Mary several times in 1858 near **Lourdes** (France). Lourdes is now a popular **pilgrimage site** — many think people can be **healed** by visiting it.

Revelation

Visions and dreams are important to some Buddhists

Some Buddhists believe that **supernatural beings** from different **realms of existence** (see p.33) can **reveal themselves** to humans on Earth. This usually happens in a **dream** or in a **vision**. These beings are also in the **cycle of samsara** and are not **enlightened**.

The most famous example of this happened to Siddhartha Gautama's **mother**, **Queen Maya**, before he was born. In a **dream**, Queen Maya saw a great **white elephant**. An elephant is a symbol of **majesty** and **authority**. The elephant **circled** her before entering her womb through the right side of her body. The next day, a wise man told the Queen that she would give birth to a **baby**, who would become a **Buddha**.

Many people don't believe in religious experiences

Religious experiences are **private**, so it's **impossible** to show **proof** of them to someone else. **Atheists** and **humanists** don't believe in God, so think religious experiences can be **explained** in **other ways**:

Some may happen because of **wish fulfilment** — the person wants the experience so **much** that their **subconscious** makes it **happen**.

→ Religious people tend to have visions **consistent** with their **own** religious beliefs, and not of **figures** or **ideas** from **another** religion, which casts **doubt** on them.

The person involved may be **lying** about their experience.

→ This could be because they might **profit** from being believed.

Some religious experiences may result from things which **affect** the **brain**, such as **mental illness**, or **physical illness** such as **brain tumours**, or **drugs**.

→ An example is the **12th century** nun **Hildegard of Bingen**, who saw visions **all her life**, but some people think she was actually suffering from **migraines**.

The person might have **misinterpreted** their experience, or chosen to interpret it in a **religious** way.

→ For example, if you were **ill** and dreamt you would be **cured** the **next day**, and the **next day** you felt much **better**, you might decide **God** was **involved** — or you might just think it a **coincidence**.

Some **believers** may **not** believe in these **experiences** either, particularly ones not **written** in their **sacred text**. They might prefer to **focus** on **God** and living a **good life** instead of events which may or may not be **true**.

Religious experiences can bring up **contradictions** in the ideas people have about God. It's hard to understand **why**, if God is **capable** of **acting** in the world, he doesn't do it **more often**. **Miracles** (see p.58) show God's **power** as they **break** the **laws of nature**, but this doesn't explain why he doesn't **use** his **power** to **prevent suffering**.

Branches of the same faith may have different views...

...so make sure you revise different opinions, as you'll often be asked to give two contrasting beliefs in the exam. Meanwhile, try this exam-style question:

Explain two religious beliefs about visions. Refer to sacred texts in your answer. [5]

Christianity & Buddhism # Arguments Against the Existence of God

Atheists *and humanists* argue there's no evidence

- Many **atheists** and **humanists** don't believe in God because they don't think there's any **evidence** he exists.
- They say **visions** and **miracles** have **scientific** or **straightforward** explanations, and aren't **proof** of a **divine being**. Many such experiences happened a **long time ago**, before science could **explain** them.

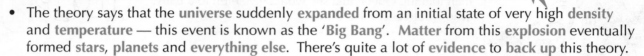

For example, some scientists believe that the **10 plagues** in **Egypt** before the **Exodus** could be explained by the eruption of a **volcano** in the **Mediterranean**, which **contradicts** the belief that **God** sent the **plagues**.

- Atheists and humanists argue that **science** provides **sufficient explanation** for the **origins** of the **universe**.

Many think the Big Bang Theory *explains* creation

- The theory says that the universe suddenly **expanded** from an initial state of very high **density** and **temperature** — this event is known as the 'Big Bang'. **Matter** from this **explosion** eventually formed **stars**, **planets** and **everything else**. There's quite a lot of **evidence** to **back up** this theory.
- However, we **don't** know what **caused** the Big Bang — so many Christians argue that it was **God** who **caused** it, which seems to fit with the 'First Cause' argument.

Evil *and suffering make people* doubt there is a God

Christians may have very **different** views on evil and suffering to **non-religious** people:

> God is **omniscient** (all-knowing), **omnipotent** (all-powerful), and **benevolent** (kind). He knows what **happens** in the world, doesn't want people to **suffer**, and is **powerful** enough to do something about it.

 vs.

> There's a lot of **suffering** in the world, which seems to **contradict** these ideas. It's hard to see how God could **allow** it to happen, so it's doubtful he exists.

> In the scriptures, suffering is often described as **punishment** for people's sins, e.g. God **destroyed** a town of people he considered **sinful**, while **sparing** a few who weren't.

 vs.

> Suffering is **widespread** and affects **everyone**, so **justifying** suffering as **punishment** doesn't make sense. It also doesn't seem to add up because **other animals** suffer too, even though they **can't** be being punished for their sins.

Believers might explain it by saying that humans need to be able to **choose** between **good** and **evil** as a test of their **character** — that's why they have **free will**. Without **bad** things happening, good **can't** exist.

Christians believe the concept of original sin can explain suffering (see p.6).
God gave people free will — they choose to create suffering or good.
- St Augustine said suffering was the price people pay for free will.
- St Irenaeus thought people were created with faults because they had to develop into being children of God — so they needed evil and suffering to exist, else they'd have no concept of what's right.
Christians try to follow God's example of goodness — Psalms 119 asks for his help to do so. God can punish those who aren't good. He isn't only responsible for good — he creates suffering as a punishment.

> **"I bring prosperity and create disaster"**
> *Isaiah 45:7*

Buddhists have a very **different attitude** to **suffering**:

- Buddhists do not struggle to explain suffering because they do not believe in an **omnibenevolent** god. The main reason we suffer is because everything is **impermanent** (see p.26). Impermanence causes **mental pain** (e.g. feeling sad about someone dying) and **physical pain** (e.g. getting arthritis from old age).
- Humans constantly **attach themselves** to things (people, objects and places) because they are unaware that these things are **impermanent**. This leads to **more suffering**.
- Humans should teach themselves about the **Three Marks of Existence** (see p.26), so they can **suffer less**.

 EXAM TIP

Revise thoroughly for the exam — else you'll suffer...

In the exam, read each question carefully. You've probably heard this a million times, but it's worth it — especially with complex topics such as these. You need to know exactly what's being asked.

Theme C — The Existence of God and Revelation

Revision Summary

A whole page of exam-style questions — just what you've been waiting for. They'll test whether you **remember** what you've learnt in the section, and get you used to what you'll be asked to do in the **exam**.

If there's anything you're not completely sure about, **go back** through the section and have another read of the relevant pages, then give the questions **another go**. There will be one question which has **extra marks** for **spelling**, **punctuation** and **grammar** — make sure you check your writing extra carefully for that one.

To get you warmed up, let's start with these 1 mark multiple choice questions.

1) Which of the following believe it's impossible to know for certain if God exists or not?
   a) Atheists   b) Humanists   c) Theologians   d) Agnostics

2) Which of the following is the theory developed by Darwin?
   a) Genesis   b) Big Bang theory   c) Theory of evolution   d) Design argument

3) Which of the following means all-powerful?
   a) Omnipotent   b) Omniscient   c) Infinite   d) Transcendent

4) Which of the following is not a type of revelation?
   a) Vision   b) God   c) Miracle   d) Scripture

You can get 2 marks for these, so make two short points in your answer.

5) Give two aspects of the First Cause argument.

6) Give two religious beliefs about special revelation.

7) Give two examples of how God's compassion might be shown through revelation.

8) Give two examples of people who have had visions.

Let's ramp it up with some 4 mark questions. Make two points and develop them further to get full marks. You need to write about the views of one or more religions.

9) Explain two contrasting religious beliefs about evolution.

10) Explain two similar religious beliefs about the scriptures as revelation.

11) Explain two similar religious beliefs about God's characteristics.

> To make sure your longer answers are clear, make sure your answer is well-structured.

For this question, you must refer to the main religious tradition in the UK and at least one other religious viewpoint. This question is worth 4 marks.

12) Explain two contrasting beliefs about the revelation of God in nature.

For top marks in these 5 mark questions, you need to refer to religious texts.

13) Explain two contrasting religious beliefs about how creation proves the existence of God.

14) Explain two contrasting religious beliefs about miracles in the scriptures.

15) Explain two contrasting religious beliefs about how God can allow evil and suffering.

Finish on a high with this 12 mark question. It has an extra 3 marks available for spelling, punctuation and grammar. Before you begin, use the bullet points in the question to make a plan and structure your answer — you'll need to include all the things the bullet points ask for in your answer. Have a quick brainstorm of arguments for and against the statement.

16) 'God doesn't exist.'
    Evaluate this statement.
    Your answer should include the following:
    • arguments that support the statement
    • arguments that disagree with the statement
    • religious arguments
    • a conclusion

> Have a look at the 'Do Well in Your Exam' section for help with writing essays.

General	**Peace and Conflict**

Peace is the absence of conflict and violence

- **Peace** means that everyone in the world lives in **harmony**, and there is **no conflict**.
- Many organisations, such as the **United Nations** (**UN**), work to find **peaceful solutions** to disputes and to **end all wars**, all over the world.
- Christianity and Buddhism both **encourage** believers to work towards **achieving peace** in the world.

Pacifism

Pacifists believe that **all** disputes should be settled **peacefully**.
- There were pacifists in Britain who **refused** to fight in the world wars.
  - Some of these '**conscientious objectors**' went to prison rather than go against their beliefs — they were **prisoners of conscience**.
  - They suffered **humiliation** in prison, and after they'd been released.
- There are different **degrees** of pacifism.
  - Some people are against violence **under any circumstances**.
  - However, others may **disagree** with violence, but understand that sometimes violence is the **least horrible** option.

> **pacifist**
> *someone who has strongly held beliefs that war and physical violence are wrong*

Violence happens for many different reasons

- **CRIME** — when criminal activity leads to violent acts, e.g. **assault** or **murder**.
- **TERRORISM** — when a person or group deliberately seeks to cause **fear** and inflict **suffering** on other people through **violence**, sometimes for **political** reasons.
- **WAR** — when two or more groups or countries **fight** one another. It's **usually** decided by **governments**.

> *The attack on the World Trade Center by the terrorist organisation al-Qaeda in New York in September 2001 was the worst terrorist attack in history.*

> War and terrorism have caused many **deaths**. Lots of religious people believe that these acts are in **direct conflict** with the **sanctity of life** argument (see p.52).

- **PROTEST** — when groups of people join together to **campaign** for a cause they support. While many protests occur **peacefully**, some protests become **violent** if protesters don't feel their views are being heard.

Wars can have many causes

Most wars have causes that are a **combination** of lots of different factors:

RELIGION — this has been the cause of many **conflicts** in the past and the present (see p.64-67).

SELF-DEFENCE — wars started to **combat** a threat from another country or to **stop** them from attacking first, e.g. a **pre-emptive strike**.

TRIBALISM — this tends to trigger wars where a **group** of people fight for their own **independent** state.

HONOUR — wars fought to defend the **honour** and **dignity** of a country, or to **save face**.

GREED/ECONOMICS — **acts of aggression** (attacking without provocation) are **condemned** by the UN, so purely economic wars driven by greed (e.g. raids and invasions to gain territory or goods) are few and far between. Economic factors still have an impact though — **poverty** and **economic imbalances** can make wars **more likely**.

RETALIATION — a war might be started in **revenge** for something, e.g. **World War One** started after Franz Ferdinand, Archduke of Austria, was **assassinated**.

---

140 million people died in wars in the 20th century...

In this section, you have to know how Christians and Buddhists view violence, weapons of mass destruction and pacifism, so make sure you know what's what.

Peace and Conflict

Some wars are seen as necessary and 'just'. Others are sometimes seen as being fought for **God**.

Many people think there can be 'just' wars

Although most people see peace as being ideal, many recognise that sometimes a war has to be fought. Just War theory is a philosophical theory that explains the conditions for a war to be classed as necessary:

- There must be a **good reason** for the war, e.g. **self-defence** or to help **innocent people** under threat.
- **All** other options have been **attempted** to avoid war.
- It must be started by a **proper authority** — such as an **elected government** or **president**.
- A war must have a reasonable chance of success.
  Fighting an **unwinnable** war is considered a **waste** of lives.
- Any **harm** caused by **fighting** the war mustn't be **as bad** as the harm it's trying to **prevent**.

There are also two conditions for fighting a war justly. These are:

1 **Discrimination** — war should **discriminate** between **combatants** and **civilians**.
It's not seen as 'just' to **deliberately** target civilians.

2 **Proportionality** — the military **advantage** gained by an attack must **outweigh** any **harm** to civilians.

Religious and non-religious people might turn to situation ethics (p.51) to decide if a war is 'just'. They'd look at all the factors, and choose what they think would most likely bring about peace.

People who fight in holy wars believe they're supported by God

A **holy war** is one where people believe that **God** is 'on their side'. Wars are mentioned in the **Old Testament**, for example.

It's worth noting that many religious people don't agree with war being fought over religion.

In the past, holy wars have been fought over **territory** or to **convert** people, e.g. the **crusades** in the 11th to 13th centuries. However, holy wars can be declared for different reasons, such as to **protect** a religion.

Religion has been a factor in **modern wars** too (though often not the only factor). E.g. although the **civil war** in Syria didn't start over religion, different Muslim denominations have fought on both sides.

Atheists and **humanists**, who don't believe in God, have **criticised** religion for causing conflict. Some atheists and humanists also identify as **pacifists**, and don't agree with conflict being used at all.

Christians believe people should be peaceful

Many of Jesus's teachings show that peace is the ultimate goal for all human beings

Isaiah 9:6 referred to the Messiah as the *"Prince of Peace"* (NIV).

Christians believe Jesus was the Messiah and God wanted him to create peace on Earth.

For Christians, Jesus's command to *"Love your enemies"* (Luke 6:27 NIV) is very important in the way they live their lives. He said that people shouldn't follow the Old Testament teachings about retaliation:

> *"You have heard that it was said, 'Eye for eye, and tooth for tooth.' But I tell you... If anyone slaps you on the right cheek, turn to them the other cheek also."* Matthew 5:38-39 NIV

This implies that Christians shouldn't meet violence with violence.

Even when Judas had betrayed him, Jesus didn't condone anyone being violent.

> *"All who draw the sword will die by the sword."* Matthew 26:52 NIV

This suggests that people who engage in conflict will die because of it.

Christianity | **Peace and Conflict**

Many Christians follow Jesus's teachings and work for peace

Some Christians put Jesus's teachings into **action** and work to put an **end** to **violence** in the world.

> **Dorothy Day** was a Catholic **activist** who followed Jesus's **pacifist** teachings. She protested against the Spanish Civil War, WW2, violence and nuclear weapons in the **USA** (see p.68). She co-founded '**The Catholic Worker**', a newspaper which was firmly **anti-war** and eventually evolved into a pacifist group of **campaigners**. She believed that Jesus's teachings mean Christians should be **pacifists**.

> Archbishop **Oscar Romero** worked for peace during turbulent times in 1970s **El Salvador**. He raised awareness of the **suffering** and **violence** people were being subjected to by the **military** and the **police**. He **helped** those affected by the cruelty, **fought** for their **rights** and **promoted peace** between opposing groups. He was killed for his beliefs in 1980.

> The Society of Friends (Quakers) is opposed to war under all circumstances.

Because of their belief in peace, Christians tend to use **passive resistance** against injustice — campaigning **without** violence:

> **Dr Martin Luther King** was a Baptist minister who dedicated his life to trying to change the way **black people** were treated in the USA. He organised **peaceful marches**, **rallies** and **boycotts**, and in 1965 blacks were given equal voting rights with whites.

> **Thomas Merton** was a Catholic monk and a famous **pacifist**. In the 1960s, his **writings** influenced many in the **civil rights movement** for racial equality and he was **against** the violence of the **Vietnam War**.

Most Christians **wouldn't** support violent protests, but some might think it's sometimes justified. For example, the quote below shows what Jesus did in protest when he saw that some people were **exploiting** the temple:

> "[He] overturned the tables of the money changers and the benches of those selling doves" *Matthew 21:12 NIV*

Some Christians recognise 'just' wars

- Although war goes **against** the teachings of **Jesus**, most Christian denominations **accept** that there can be such a thing as a '**just**' war (see p.65 for a reminder on the **Just War** theory).

- Some interpret this verse as meaning the government has the **right** to use **violence** to ensure peace:

> "...if you do wrong, be afraid, for rulers do not bear the sword for no reason. They are God's servants, agents of wrath to bring punishment on the wrongdoer." *Romans 13:4 NIV*

- The Catholic Church has **traditionally** accepted Just War theory:

> "Legitimate defence can be not only a right but a grave duty for one who is responsible for the lives of others." *Catechism of the Catholic Church 2265*

Holy wars are now rejected by nearly all Christians

- In the past, holy wars were fought to **convert** other people to Christianity. Jesus told his disciples:

> "Do not suppose that I have come to bring peace to the earth. I did not come to bring peace, but a sword." *Matthew 10:34 NIV*

> Many think Jesus actually meant that spreading the **Christian message** would cause **divisions** between believers and non-believers.

In the 11th, 12th and 13th centuries, Christians went on **crusades** to 'free' the Christian holy places in **Palestine**. The wars caused a lot of **devastation**.

- The **vast majority** of Christians **don't believe** in the idea of a holy war any more.
  - In fact, the Catholic Church is **reconsidering** its stance on war (see above) due to the **advanced weaponry** and **horrendous** impact of modern-day war.
- Christians are strongly **against** the indiscriminate killing involved in **terrorism**.

EXAM TIP

I'll give you a peace of advice...

For 12 mark questions, both religious and non-religious opinions will help you get top marks.

Peace and Conflict

Buddhists believe that people should be peaceful

Buddhism is a religion which promotes **peace** and **non-violence** — Buddhists believe that conflict leads to **suffering**:

* Violence goes against the **First Moral Precept** (do not harm or kill).
* Buddhists follow the **Dhamma** in order to **reduce suffering**. **Violence** always leads to **suffering** and so Buddhists try to avoid it at all costs.
* The **Buddha** taught that people should give up the desire to fight, even for **self-defence**. Because of this, many Buddhists would call themselves **pacifists** because they believe violence can never be justified.

> **"Even if bandits were to savagely sever you, limb by limb [...] whoever of you harbours ill will at heart would not be upholding my Teaching."**
> *Kakacupama Sutta, The Parable of the Saw*

Ahimsa
* Ahimsa means **non-harm**. It is a concept Buddhism shares with Hinduism and other **Indian religions**.
* Many Buddhists practise ahimsa by avoiding harming **living things** in all areas of their life, e.g. by being **vegetarian**.
* Some Buddhists believe ahimsa means harming things is **always wrong** and so **violence** can never be **justified**.

Peaceful protests
* Buddhists usually use **peaceful protest** as a means of fighting **injustice**.
* For example, in 2005, the **Buddhist Peace Fellowship** (an organisation dedicated to non-violent protest) released **peace lanterns** into the air and held **lectures** to protest against the **Iraq War**.

Some Buddhists think violence can be used in self-defence

Some Buddhists think that it's acceptable to use violence to defend yourself:

* Some Buddhists practise martial arts in order to protect themselves.
* Shaolin is a martial art developed by Buddhist monks. It is only to be used in self-defence and never as a form of attack. The person practising shaolin is only allowed to use the amount of force necessary to protect themselves and no more.

* Despite Buddhism's clear principles of non-violence, there are examples of Buddhists justifying war and violence around the world. This is because religion and politics often get mixed up.
* For example, in Sri Lanka, there was a civil war between Buddhists and Hindus that lasted from 1983 to 2009. Both Hindus and Buddhists may have used self-defence to justify their fighting.

! However, Buddhists are generally against acts of **terrorism**, as these involve being the **attacker** rather than the **defender**.

Buddhism clearly teaches that violence is wrong...
Write down three reasons why Christians might be opposed to violence and two examples of when some Christians might see violence as justified. Then do the same for Buddhism.

Christianity & Buddhism

Weapons of Mass Destruction

Make sure you know what Christians and Buddhists think about weapons of mass destruction.

Weapons of mass destruction *cause a huge amount of damage*

- Weapons of mass destruction (WMDs) can destroy large areas of land and kill lots of people all at once.
- They're indiscriminate — they harm soldiers and civilians alike.
- There are several types of WMDs, including: **nuclear** **chemical** **biological**

There are many arguments for and against possessing nuclear weapons:

Banned by international law — using them is a **war crime**.

Views FOR possessing nuclear weapons	Views AGAINST

• Nuclear weapons serve as a **deterrent** to ensure peace — a country might **not** attack another if that country has nuclear weapons.
   • E.g. in the 20th century, several conflicts were **settled** or **sidestepped** because nuclear weapons posed too big a **risk**.
• Some have a **utilitarian** perspective — the best course of action is the one that brings about the best **balance** of positive and negative results.
   • E.g. the USA bombed Hiroshima and Nagasaki in Japan in WW2 as they thought that using nuclear weapons would **save** the most **lives** overall, and **end** the war **faster**.
• Nuclear weapons could be used by a country in order to **defend** itself if under attack.
	• Nuclear weapons are **costly**. **Funds** could be **better spent**, e.g. on healthcare.
	• **Widespread suffering** caused by these weapons goes against the 'sanctity of life' argument (p.52) and the First Moral Precept (p.34).
	• Believers who agree with Just War theory might argue that the indiscriminate nature of nuclear weapons (they would kill innocent people) could **never** be classed as **just**.
	• Earth is God's creation — using nuclear weapons would **destroy** what God trusted humans to take **care** of.

Many religious believers are *against WMDs*

Christian views

 Some Christians use Jesus's teachings about peace to argue against nuclear weapons. All Christian denominations are against using them.

 Christians might turn to Deuteronomy 20:

> "When you lay siege to a city for a long time... do not destroy its trees by putting an axe to them, because you can eat their fruit." *Deuteronomy 20:19 NIV*

This suggests that women and children should be spared, and unnecessary damage shouldn't be caused. The total destruction that WMDs would cause goes against this.

 Some think nuclear weapons help to keep the peace as countries are afraid of starting a nuclear war.

Buddhist views

 WMDs go against the First Moral Precept and cause suffering on a large scale. Because of this, Buddhists are usually against the use of them and against having them as a deterrent.

 Tibetan Buddhists might turn to the teachings of the Dalai Lama (leader of Tibetan Buddhists). He visited Hiroshima, in Japan (the site of a nuclear bombing), to speak about the dangers of WMDs.

> "The message from here to all the world is that nuclear weapons are terrible." *Dalai Lama, 2006*

- Some atheists are in favour of WMDs to deter an opponent and to potentially use — they don't believe their actions will be judged.
- Others are strongly anti-WMDs as they believe people only live one life on Earth.
- Humanists have opposed the use of WMDs due to the huge number of people that would suffer.

 EXAM QUESTION

Make sure you know arguments for and against WMDs...

Explain two contrasting religious beliefs about nuclear weapons. [4]

Peacemaking

Finding peace and resolving conflicts is **important** to Christians and Buddhists.

Justice, forgiveness **and** *reconciliation* **are key to** *peacemaking*

Justice	**Justice** is the idea of each person getting what they **deserve**, and maintaining what's **right**. **Christians** think that God is **just** — he treats and judges people **fairly** as he created everyone **equally**. Justice leads to a **fairer society** — if people feel they're treated equally, there's more chance of **peace**. **Buddhists** believe that the person will receive **bad karma** as a consequence of their actions, which could be considered justice.

Forgiveness	**Forgiveness** is when a person **stops** feeling **resentment** or **anger** towards someone who has caused them to **suffer**. As God is merciful towards them, **Christians** feel that they should **forgive** other people, and that forgiveness is the **only** way true peace can be achieved. Buddhists may feel that forgiveness is **unnecessary**, as by practising compassion and loving kindness they may **avoid feeling resentment** in the first place.

Reconciliation	**Reconciliation** is bringing people together that previously were in conflict, to make **peace**.

Christians **believe that God is** *fair* **and** *forgiving*

Christians believe that **justice** is very important, since people are **equal** in the eyes of God.
They have a **duty** to look after other people, and try to **guide** them to do what's right and **repent** of their sins.

> "...what does the Lord require of you?
> To act justly and to love mercy and to walk
> humbly with your God." *Micah 6:8 NIV*

They believe they should follow God's **example** and be just to **others**. The parable of the **sheep** and **goats** shows God treats people well if they've done the same to others.

Forgiveness is important to Christians (see p.75 for more about it). They believe they should seek God's forgiveness and forgive people who've hurt them.

> "Blessed are the merciful, for they will
> be shown mercy." *Matthew 5:7 NIV*

If they **repent**, and put their **faith** in God, God **forgives** people and they are **reconciled** with him.
Christians believe the same sort of **reconciliation** is needed between people to create peace.

Buddhists **believe that all** *actions* **have** *consequences*

- Buddhists do not believe in holding on to **negative feelings** towards others. Instead, Buddhists try to have **loving kindness** (see p.33) towards everyone.

- Buddhists believe that everyone's actions have **consequences** for themselves through the good or bad **karma** they produce.

- Most Buddhists think that fighting for justice can be achieved **peacefully** through **non-violent protest** or **reconciliation**, e.g. the Dalai Lama proposed peace talks in 1988 between the Tibetans and the Chinese.

REVISION TASK

Learn it all — the examiner isn't as forgiving as God...

Draw a grid on some paper. Down one side, write 'Christianity' and 'Buddhism'. Along the top, write 'Justice', 'Forgiveness' and 'Reconciliation'. Fill it in with what you've learned on this page.

Christianity & Buddhism

Peacemaking

Many religious organisations work towards **peace** and help people in countries devastated by war.

Religious believers **can work for peace** *directly* **and** *indirectly*

Many religious believers feel they must act to create **peace** — see p.66 for some examples.
People can work for peace either **directly** or **indirectly**.

E.g. working with or for organisations which offer **relief** to war-torn areas.

E.g. **donating** money to charitable causes, holding **protests** and **demonstrations** against conflicts, working to ensure that people have equal **human rights** (which could help to **avoid** conflict).

Christian charities **work for** *peace* **and help** *victims* **of** *war*

Many feel that it's important to **help people** caught up in **conflict zones** and to try to bring **peace** to the area. In the **Sermon on the Mount**, Jesus says:

> **"Blessed are the peacemakers, for they will be called children of God."** *Matthew 5:9 NIV*

Some religious **charities** exist to help achieve peace. They **campaign** for help for groups in conflict to **rebuild** their **relationship**, or assist people in **war-torn areas**.

Christian Aid is a charity that works to reduce poverty. It has urged governments to find a **compromise** in the Israel/Palestine conflict.

Pax Christi is a Catholic organisation that works for peaceful conflict **resolution**. Read more about it in the last section of p.21.

Tearfund® helps people who are refugees from war-torn areas. They help people in the short term by giving them some food and somewhere to stay. However, they also help people to get back on their feet permanently by teaching them valuable skills they can use to support themselves.

Buddhists **work for peace** *in the world*

Buddhists try to show **compassion** in all situations.
This includes **helping people** who are living in areas of **conflict**.

Buddhist Global Relief is a charity dedicated to providing **aid** to those in need. For example, one of their past projects provided **food** and **education** for **girls** during a conflict in **Bangladesh**.

The 14th **Dalai Lama, Tenzin Gyatso**, was awarded the **Nobel Peace Prize** in 1989 for his peaceful attempt to reconcile the relationship between **China** and **Tibet**. This included his **Five Point Peace Plan**, which aimed to turn Tibet into an **area of peace**.

Peace, love, charity... and a nice revision task to end with...

How do religious believers work for a more peaceful world? Jot down as many ways as you can.

Revision Summary

That was a lot of information to take in there, so now **test yourself** to see how you got on. These questions are similar to the ones that you'll be answering in the **exam**, so you know what it'll be like on the day.

If there's anything you can't answer, go back through the section and have **another go** when you've **re-read** it. For some questions — you'll be told which ones — there are **extra marks** for **spelling, punctuation** and **grammar**, so check your writing carefully.

The exam will start with some nice 1 mark multiple choice questions.

1) Which of the following is the act of deliberately causing suffering and fear through violence?
   a) Passive resistance   b) Pacifism   c) Holy war   d) Terrorism ☑

2) Which of the following is starting a war in revenge for something?
   a) Tribalism   b) Retaliation   c) Self-defence   d) Honour ☑

3) Which of the following is the idea that everyone should get what they deserve?
   a) Justice   b) Peacemaking   c) Reconciliation   d) Forgiveness ☑

4) Which of the following is the concept of non-harm shared by many Indian religions?
   a) Shaolin   b) Dhamma   c) Ahimsa   d) Karma ☑

Moving up to 2 marks now, no biggy. 2 short points are all you need.

5) Give two religious beliefs about terrorism. ☑

6) Give two examples of individuals who have worked for peace. ☑

7) Give two religious beliefs about violent protest. ☑

8) Give two religious beliefs about reconciliation. ☑

4 marks now — make 2 points, but this time develop them for full marks.

9) Explain two similar religious beliefs about justice. ☑

10) Explain two similar religious beliefs about forgiveness. ☑

For these questions, you must refer to the main religious tradition in the UK and at least one other religious viewpoint. They're both worth 4 marks.

11) Explain two contrasting beliefs in Britain today about violence. ☑

12) Explain two contrasting beliefs in Britain today about pacifism. ☑

Make sure your writing is well structured and accurate in the longer questions — your points have to be clear to the examiner.

Next you'll face some 5 mark questions. You need to refer to religious texts in order to get all 5 marks.

13) Explain two religious beliefs about the importance of peace. ☑

14) Explain two religious beliefs about just war. ☑

15) Explain two religious beliefs about holy war. ☑

16) Explain two religious beliefs about how peace can be achieved. ☑

Hang on to your hat — it's the 12 mark question (plus 3 extra marks for SPaG). The question will come with a list of things to include, so use it when you start planning your answer. Write a list of arguments for and against the statement and make sure you've included them all.

17) 'It is justified for a country to possess nuclear weapons.'
    Evaluate this statement.
    Your answer should include the following:
    • religious arguments to support the statement
    • religious arguments that disagree with the statement
    • a conclusion
    You can also include non-religious points of view in your answer.

If you need advice on writing essays, have a look at the 'Do Well in Your Exam' section.

☑

Theme D — Religion, Peace and Conflict

Christianity & Buddhism

Religion and the Law

Most religions teach people to **follow** the **law**, but some people think that religious law should take **priority**.

Religions *teach people* how to *live their lives*

CHRISTIANITY teaches people to live **good lives**. This includes **following** religious **teachings**, e.g. by helping other people.

😊 The good things that people do will **please God**.

People should **avoid** sin and evil, as their actions will be **judged** when they die.

The **sheep** and **goats** parable (Matthew 25:31-46) says that everyone will be **judged** and **separated** into the **good** (the sheep) and the **bad** (the goats). Jesus said that **helping** another person is like helping **him**. If you **ignore** someone in need of help, it's like **ignoring him**.

> "...whatever you did **not do for one of the least of these, you did not do for me**"
> *Matthew 25:45 NIV*

Many Christians believe that **evil** is caused by humans **misusing** their **free will** — they believe that the **original sin** people are born with makes them **capable** of sin (see p.6). Some say **Satan** tempts people to sin.

BUDDHISTS follow the **Dhamma**. The Dhamma is the teachings the **Buddha** gave while he was alive. The most important of these is the **Four Noble Truths** (see pages 29-30).

Buddhists do not believe actions are inherently **good** or **evil**, but that all of our actions have **consequences** through **karma**. Following the **Eightfold Path** (the fourth Noble Truth) will produce **good karma** and reduce **suffering**, but other actions (e.g. going against the **Five Moral Precepts**) will produce **bad karma**.

Bad karma is a result of the **Three Poisons** (ignorance, greed and hate), which are caused by **human desire**.

Law *is essential* to most societies

State
- The **laws of the state** define what's **right** and **wrong**, though this can **differ** from **religious ideas**.
- Most nations believe that the **rule of law** is the best way of **protecting** people in society. Without law there's the risk of **chaos**. With it, people know what they **can** and **cannot** do.
- In the UK, **laws** are rules made by Parliament and **enforced** by the courts.

Religious
- Religions such as Christianity teach that **God** has commanded people to follow law. But some religious believers think that **religious law** is more important than the **laws of the land**.
- Where religious law and state law **disagree** some believers think it's better to commit a **crime** if it means they avoid committing a **sin**.

For **CHRISTIANS**, there's a difference between a **sin** and a **crime**. A **sin** is when **religious** law is broken, i.e. when God's teaching is disobeyed. A **crime** is when the **state** laws are broken.

Christians have a **duty** to look after **other people**, and try to **guide** them to do what's right and **repent** of their sins — **justice** is important.

justice
the idea of each person getting what they deserve (including punishing the guilty) and maintaining what's right.

BUDDHISTS follow the **Dhamma** — the teachings of the Buddha. The **Eightfold Path** gives them specific guidance about how to live their lives, e.g. having the right **livelihood**.

Buddhists do not believe that going against the Buddha's teaching is a **sin** (sin is a Christian concept), but they do believe each person's actions will be reflected in the **karma** they produce. E.g. having a livelihood that causes others to **suffer** will produce **bad karma** and this could affect the outcome of that person's **rebirth** (see p.33).

REVISION TASK

Learn about the law — and that's an order...

Write a short summary about what each religion teaches about good and evil.

Crime

Crime happens on a **daily** basis for many reasons, and it can take many **different forms**.

Many crimes break religious laws and teachings

There are many **different types** of crime, including **murder**, **theft** and **hate crimes**.

hate crime
any type of crime committed against someone because of their ethnicity, religion, etc.

MURDER

Murder, often seen as the **worst** crime, goes against the Christian idea of **sanctity of life** (the belief that life is **sacred**). It also goes against the **First Moral Precept** in Buddhism — do not harm a living thing.

Christianity and Buddhism are against all three crimes as they break **religious moral laws**.

Christians are strongly against **murder** and **theft** as they **break** two of the **Ten Commandments**.

The **Buddha** taught that attaching yourself to **material things** causes **suffering** because these things are **impermanent**.

HATE CRIME

THEFT

Hate crimes cause **suffering** and do not reflect the Buddhist concept of **loving kindness**.

Theft and **hate crimes** disregard Christian teachings that people should be treated **equally**, as the offender shows **no concern** for the victim.

Crime is caused by lots of different factors

Most religious believers would agree that if someone does something **illegal**, they **deserve** to be **punished**. But the cause of crime **isn't** as simple as someone just being **bad** — there are many different **reasons** why a person might **commit a crime**:

POVERTY — People who are poor might turn to **crime** out of **desperation**. They might **steal food** or **money**, or earn **money** illegally, e.g. by selling stolen goods.

UPBRINGING — Some people might become criminals if they've had a **troubled childhood**, or if they've **grown up** around crime and it's become **normal** to them.

MENTAL ILLNESS — This can lead people to commit crimes because, e.g., they may not fully **understand** the **difference** between what's **legal** and **illegal**. Others may be easily **persuaded** into committing a crime.

ADDICTION — Being dependent on something such as **drugs** or **alcohol** can lead to people doing illegal things to **fund** their **addiction**.

GREED — Someone might **steal** or **earn** money **illegally** to get something they **want** but can't afford.

HATE — A person might do something illegal because someone else has **treated** them **badly**, or because they're driven by **prejudice**, e.g. racism.

OPPOSITION TO UNJUST LAW — A law might be **broken** as a **protest** if it's seen as unfair. In the 1950s and 60s many people, such as **Rosa Parks**, broke laws that treated black people **unfairly** in the **USA**.

Many feel that the **reason** behind the crime should be taken into **consideration**, and many religious people want to **help** the **individual** as well as tackle the **bigger issues** that cause crime. However, certain causes would be more likely to get **sympathy** than others, e.g. **poverty** would be seen as a more **acceptable** reason than **greed**. Many think that breaking a law that is **unfair** or that goes **against** religious law is **acceptable**.

Theme E — Religion, Crime and Punishment

| Christianity & Buddhism | **Crime** |

Religions tend to **oppose** criminal actions, and many **religious organisations** work to put an **end** to them.

Christians **work to prevent crimes**

Christians are **strongly against** crime — they're told to **care** for others.

> "Love your neighbour as yourself" *Mark 12:31 NIV*

- Committing a crime such as **theft** or a **hate crime** doesn't treat the victim as an **equal**.
- Murder is seen as **destroying** something **created** by God.

> "We must obey God rather than human beings!" *Acts 5:29 NIV*

- Christians have **defied laws** to fight for what's **right**, e.g. Martin Luther King (see p.66). In this case, Christians may **support** breaking laws.
- Many Christians would **help** people who are, e.g., struggling in **poverty**, in order to tackle the **source** of crime. They might donate to **charity** or help out in **food banks**, among other things.
- **Christian groups** also play their part to try to **prevent** crime. **Street Pastors**, who help people out at night (see p.20), have helped to **lower** crime rates and **prevent violence**.

> The **Prison Fellowship** is a Christian organisation in England and Wales that helps prisoners by **praying** for them and through **group activities** and maintaining **contact** with their **families**. They try to make prisoners see how they have **affected victims** of their crimes and **stop** them from **committing crime** again when they leave prison, e.g. through **restorative justice** (see p.75).

Buddhists **want to prevent suffering for all**

- If a Buddhist chooses to **commit a crime**, then they are not following the **Eightfold Path**. This is because it teaches Buddhists to make the **right action** (not harm others) and to have the **right speech** (always be honest).
- Buddhists believe in showing **compassion** in all circumstances, and this includes towards **criminals**.
- Some Buddhist organisations and services aim to **prevent crime** and stop criminals from **reoffending**:

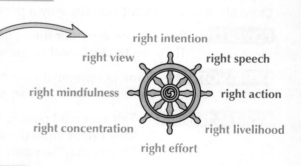

The Buddhist Global Relief Fund

The Buddhist Global Relief Fund is a Buddhist organisation that helps **prevent crime** by providing **aid** and **educational opportunities** to people living in **poverty** all over the world.

Angulimala

Angulimala is a British Buddhist **chaplaincy service** that provides **guidance** and **advice** to people who have recently **left prison**. This helps reduce the chances of them **reoffending**.

There's lots to learn here, so have another read if you need...

'To prevent crime, we should tackle poverty.' Evaluate this statement. Include religious arguments that support and disagree with the statement in your answer. [12]

Theme E — Religion, Crime and Punishment

Forgiveness

Make sure you know some different **religious views** about **forgiveness**.

Forgiveness can reunite people and prevent reoffending

Forgiveness means stopping being **angry** with someone who's done something **wrong**. Many Christians believe God is **merciful** towards people who **genuinely** seek his **mercy** and that they should **reflect** God's forgiving nature in their **own behaviour**.

Many believe forgiveness is important, so that...

...criminals can be **reconciled** with the **community**. If they leave prison **isolated** from others, with **no job** and **little prospects**, **reoffending** might seem like the **only option**. Forgiveness allows **both** victims and perpetrators to **move on**.

Forgiveness can be **shown** in many ways. **Lesser offences** no longer stay on people's **records permanently**, and there are **schemes** that give ex-offenders **skills** and a **job** when they're released.

Restorative justice can help people forgive

Restorative justice is where an offender might **meet** people who've **suffered** because of the crime they committed. Actually meeting the people they've hurt can help offenders to **realise** the **extent** of the **damage** they've done, try to **make up for** their actions and **discourage** them from **reoffending**. It helps the **victim** to work towards **forgiving** the offender.

! However, many religious people believe that **criminals** should still be **punished** for what they've done.

Christianity teaches that forgiveness comes from love

- Jesus taught that **God** is always ready to **forgive** and that Christians must **accept** that forgiveness, and forgive **others** in turn. The **Lord's Prayer** includes a verse about forgiveness (Matthew 6:12).

- Jesus told people to seek **reconciliation** in any disagreements **before** offering a **gift** to God at the temple:

> **"First go and be reconciled to them; then come and offer your gift."** *Matthew 5:24 NIV*

- He also taught people to forgive *"not seven times, but seventy-seven times"* (Matthew 18:22 NIV).

- Forgiveness is closely related to **repentance**. Christians believe that God's forgiveness can only come when they **repent** of their sins (i.e. say sorry, and turn their backs on their sins).

Buddhists believe in showing loving kindness to all

- Buddhists try to have **loving kindness** (see p.33) towards everyone, including **criminals**.

- Holding on to feelings of **hate** or **revenge** will only lead to more **suffering**. Buddhists should let go of any **attachments** they have to these feelings in order to feel **peace** within themselves.

- Everyone's actions have **consequences** through the good or bad **karma** they produce.

> **"Let him radiate boundless love towards the entire world — above, below, and across — unhindered, without ill will, without enmity."** *Sutta Nipata, Metta Sutta*

Forgive and forget (but not your revision)...

Explain two religious beliefs about forgiveness. You should include sacred text references. [5]

Theme E — Religion, Crime and Punishment

General, Christianity & Buddhism	# Punishment

Punishment can be used to 'get back' at someone for committing a crime, or to **prevent** crime in the future.

Punishment can have various aims

Punishment is **needed** in society so that people **follow** the law. Criminals should face the **consequences** for their actions and victims should get **justice**. Punishment has many **purposes**:

Retribution
Some people think of punishment as a way of taking **revenge** on a criminal, of making them 'pay' for what they've done. Critics of this way of thinking argue that revenge **doesn't put right** the wrong — that it's better to look for a more **constructive** solution.

Protection
If a criminal is considered **dangerous**, then their punishment should **protect** the rest of **society**, e.g. imprisonment. Not many people would disagree with this, but some would argue that you protect society best by **reforming** offenders.

Reformation
Punishment should aim to **change** criminals so they won't offend again — the idea being that nobody is inherently **bad**. Many Christians feel this allows offenders to **repent** and seek **forgiveness** from God for their actions. Programmes to reform criminals include **counselling** and giving them **work** in the community.

Deterrence
This is the idea that if a punishment is sufficiently **bad** in some way (e.g. expensive, embarrassing, restricting, painful) it will **put people off** committing the crime because they understand the **consequences**. Critics argue that people don't **stop to think** about punishment before they commit a crime, especially if they've taken drugs or alcohol, so deterrence **doesn't work**.

There are various Christian views on the aims of punishment

- Christians think that criminals should be **punished** for what they've done in a **just** way.

 Some think punishment should be *"eye for eye"* (Leviticus 24:20 NIV), so focus on **retribution**.

 Others believe they should *"turn... the other cheek"* (Matthew 5:39 NIV), and so look more towards **reformation**.

- Being **merciful** is important in Christianity, and Christians believe **reformation** is **important**.

> *"...if someone is caught in a sin, you who live by the Spirit should restore that person gently."*
> *Galatians 6:1 NIV*

- Christians also value **deterrence** and **protection** — these help make communities **less dangerous**.

- Jesus told people to look at their **own behaviour** before **criticising** others. In John 8, a woman who was accused of **adultery** was **saved** by Jesus when he said:

> **"Let any one of you who is without sin be the first to throw a stone at her."** *John 8:7 NIV*

No-one did, and it reminds Christians that **everyone sins**.

Buddhists believe that actions have consequences through karma

AGAINST punishment	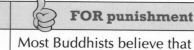 FOR punishment
Some Buddhists believe it **isn't necessary** to punish another person because their actions will already have **consequences** in the **karma** they produce. If a person has caused others to **suffer**, they will have produced **bad karma**, which will affect their rebirth. **Angulimala** is a famous figure in Buddhism. He was a **criminal** who **murdered** hundreds of people, but later **changed his behaviour** and became a **follower** of the Buddha and a **good man**. The Buddha **did not punish** Angulimala, but instead taught him to follow the **Dhamma**.	Most Buddhists believe that punishment in this life **is necessary**, but that the aim of punishment should be **reformation**. **Buddha-nature** is the view that all humans can become **enlightened** if they live the right kind of life. This means everyone can change, including **criminals**.

Punishment

Punishments **vary** according to the crime, and religious believers hold **different views** on these punishments.

There are many different *types* of punishment

Depending on the **severity** of the **crime** committed, criminals can be given **various sentences**, including **prison**, **community service** and (in countries where it's legal) **corporal punishment**.

 Some religious people believe community service allows the offender to **repay** their **debt** to society yet still lead a **normal life**, which should help to **ensure** they don't **reoffend**.

Corporal punishment is **not** used in **Europe**, but it is used **elsewhere** in the world.

Some people might argue that corporal punishment and the suffering it causes would put people off reoffending. Some think that life in prison should be difficult in order to make offenders think twice about crime. They might also think that treating prisoners harshly can be more effective in reforming them.

Prisoners have **human rights** — many argue corporal punishment goes **against** this and promotes **violence**.

corporal punishment *when a criminal is punished through physical pain delivered by, e.g., beating or flogging them.*

Christians are mostly against corporal punishment

FOR corporal punishment	AGAINST corporal punishment
• There are **examples** in the **Bible** of corporal punishment being used on criminals (e.g. Deuteronomy 25:2), so it's **acceptable** in some situations. • The Bible can be seen to suggest that **disciplining** children through **corporal punishment** is **allowed**: *"Whoever spares the rod hates their children." Proverbs 13:24 NIV*	• Christians believe that prisoners have the **right** to be treated **fairly** — many want **better conditions** in prison and visit **offenders** in prison. *"Speak up and judge fairly; defend the rights of the poor and needy." Proverbs 31:9 NIV* • The **majority** of Christians are **strongly against** corporal punishment — Jesus was against violence: *"all who draw the sword will die by the sword." Matthew 26:52 NIV* • Many **disagree** with corporal punishment as it goes against the idea of Christian **compassion**.

Buddhists believe in showing compassion to everyone

• Corporal punishment goes against the **First Moral Precept** — do not harm or kill a **living thing**.
• Buddhists try to act **compassionately** in all circumstances. Corporal punishment only causes **more suffering** and does not solve the problem. Buddhists are always trying to **reduce suffering** — even the suffering of criminals.

"Hatred is never appeased by hatred in this world. By non-hatred alone is hatred appeased. This is a law eternal." Dhammapada

  Don't do the crime if you can't do the time...
You must learn views from Christianity and Buddhism on corporal punishment.

The Death Penalty

The death penalty is **killing** someone as punishment for a crime — it's also called **capital punishment**.

The death penalty isn't used much nowadays

- Capital punishment has been **abolished** in many countries, including most of Europe and South America. Elsewhere, it only tends to be used for **very serious** crimes, e.g. **murder**, **espionage** (spying) and **treason**.
- **Religious** and **non-religious** people might make some of these **arguments** for and against the death penalty:

FOR the death penalty

- The risk of death might act as a **better deterrent** to violent criminals than a prison sentence.
- If you execute a murderer, it's **impossible** for them to **kill again**. Imprisoned murderers have been known to **order** killings from jail, or to **reoffend** when released on parole. In cases like these, the **suffering** of the criminal could potentially **protect** many people.
- **Utilitarianism** (or the **principle of utility**) is the idea that the **best** course of action creates the best **balance** of **good** and **bad** results, e.g. it could be used to argue that killing criminals, although bad for them, would be good for the **majority** of society.

AGAINST the death penalty

- Killing as punishment is **just as bad** as murder — many **religious people** and **Humanists** are against **any** form of killing.
- It doesn't give the offender the chance to **reform**.
- There have been cases where someone has been proved **innocent after** having been executed.
- Life is **special** and should be **preserved** — many religious people believe in the **sanctity of life**.
- Many religious believers think **God alone** can decide when to **end** someone's **life**.

✝ **Christians** might be against the death penalty because the **Ten Commandments** forbid killing.

BUT... ...some people might use **situation ethics** to decide on a **case-by-case** basis if the death penalty should be applied. This could lead to people being **for** the death penalty in **some** cases, but **against** it in **others**, depending on, e.g., the **severity** of the crime and the **background** to the case.

Christians have mixed views on capital punishment

 Many **Christians** are opposed to **capital punishment**, as it doesn't allow for **reform**, or show **mercy**. **Jesus** said to set aside *"eye for eye"* (Matthew 5:38 NIV) and to *"love your enemies"* (Matthew 5:44 NIV).

Many are against the **violent nature** of the death penalty.

However, some Christians in the **United States** (where capital punishment is **legal**) believe that the death penalty is a **good** thing. They say it **protects** the innocent. They might refer to **biblical texts** such as:

> **"Anyone who strikes a person with a fatal blow is to be put to death."** *Exodus 21:12 NIV*

> **"Whoever sheds human blood, by humans shall their blood be shed."** *Genesis 9:6 NIV*

Capital punishment goes against the First Moral Precept

There is **no support** for capital punishment within Buddhist sacred texts. Buddhists believe killing produces **bad karma**, as it goes against the **First Moral Precept**.

The concept of **ahimsa** means **non-harm**. Buddhists try to live their lives without causing **harm** to other **living things**. Because of this, many Buddhists think that **violence** towards others can **never be justified**.

Capital punishment goes against the idea of **loving kindness** — wishing **happiness** towards all humans. Buddhists try to let go of feelings of **hatred**, **dislike** or **revenge**, and wish **peace** to all.

EXAM TIP

Learn contrasting views on the death penalty for the exam...
You must know views from Christianity and Buddhism about the death penalty.

Revision Summary

And that wraps up another section — time to see how you got on. The **questions** below are the **same style** as the questions you'll be answering in the **actual exam**.

If there's anything you can't answer, **go back** through the section and have **another go** when you've **re-read it**. For some questions — you'll be told which ones — there are **extra marks** for **spelling**, **punctuation** and **grammar**, so check your writing carefully.

Jumping right in with some 1 mark multiple choice questions.

1) Which of the following is where an offender might meet their victim?
   a) Reconciliation   b) Restorative justice   c) Community service   d) Prison

2) Which of the following is the idea that punishment should try to change the criminal for the better?
   a) Protection   b) Reformation   c) Retribution   d) Deterrence

3) Which of the following is when a criminal is punished by being subjected to physical pain?
   a) Corporal punishment   b) Hate crime   c) Capital punishment   d) Retribution

4) Which of the following is the idea that the best action is the one with the best balance of good and bad?
   a) Sanctity of life   b) Situation ethics   c) Utilitarianism   d) Compensation

For these 2 mark questions, keep it short and snappy with 2 brief points.

5) Give two religious beliefs about the laws of the state.

6) Give two examples of causes of crime.

7) Give two ways that religious people can help to prevent crime.

8) Give two arguments against capital punishment.

It's a similar idea with these 4 mark questions, but this time develop your points a bit more.

9) Explain two similar religious beliefs about breaking unjust laws.

10) Explain two similar religious beliefs about preventing crime.

11) Explain two similar religious beliefs about prison as a form of punishment.

Make sure your longer answers are well organised and clearly written so the examiner can easily see your points.

For this question, you must refer to the main religious tradition in the UK and at least one other religious viewpoint. This is worth 4 marks.

12) Explain two contrasting religious beliefs about corporal punishment.

And the questions continue — this time for 5 marks. Refer to sacred texts for full marks.

13) Explain two religious beliefs about why people should live good lives.

14) Explain two religious beliefs about murder.

15) Explain two religious beliefs about retribution as an aim of punishment.

16) Explain two religious beliefs about reformation as an aim of punishment.

Saving the best for last — the 12 mark question with 3 additional marks for SPaG. The question will have a list of information that you need to include, so use it to make a plan. Jot down arguments for and against the statement so you don't forget any when you actually start writing your answer.

17) 'The death penalty is never a suitable punishment.'
    Evaluate this statement.
    Your answer should include the following:
    • religious arguments that support the statement
    • religious arguments that disagree with the statement
    • a conclusion
    You can also include non-religious points of view in your answer.

Head over to the 'Do Well in Your Exam' section for help with writing essays.

Attitudes to Equality

You need to be aware of **different views** in **British society** for this **whole section**. You need to be able to give **Christian** views on the **status** of **women** in **religion**, as well as views on this from **one** other **religious tradition**.

Prejudice and discrimination prevent equality

> Difference in wealth is another form of inequality — see p.86.

- **Prejudice** relates to the **views** a person holds — discrimination happens when they **act** on those views:

> **prejudice**
> *judging something or someone for no good reason, or without full knowledge of a situation.*

> **discrimination**
> *treating someone unjustly or differently, often because of prejudice*

- **Prejudice** comes in **different forms**, e.g.:

> **sexism**
> *the belief one gender is inferior to the other*

> **racism**
> *prejudice against people of other races*

> **homophobia**
> *prejudice against people who are homosexual*

- The **Equality Act 2010** says it's **illegal** to **discriminate** on the grounds of '**protected characteristics**', which include race, gender, age and sexual orientation. The Act aims to ensure everyone is treated **equally**.

- **Positive discrimination** may be used when assessing **job applications** made by people from groups that are often discriminated against — it's only legal if they're **as well qualified** as the other applicants.

> **positive discrimination**
> *when someone in a group that often suffers discrimination is given an advantage.*

Christianity teaches equality

"*Do to others what you would have them do to you*" is a fundamental part of Christian teaching, often called the 'Golden Rule'. Many Christians think everyone was created equal, so they try to avoid discrimination.

> **"Love your neighbour as yourself."** *Mark 12:31 NIV*

Jesus said that this is the second most important commandment, after loving God.

> **"A new command I give you: love one another."** *John 13:34 NIV*

i.e. don't mistreat others.

> **"...discrimination ... on the grounds of sex, race, colour, social conditions, language, or religion must be ... eradicated as incompatible with God's design."** *Catechism of the Catholic Church 1935*

> The **Good Samaritan** parable is an important teaching on **prejudice**. Two **holy** men **ignore** a man who's been **beaten** and **robbed**. He's then **helped** by a **Samaritan**, a group who were **despised** at the time. The story shows how **prejudices** can be **wrong**.

Buddhists believe that all humans suffer

- Buddhists try to show **compassion** and practise **loving kindness** towards **all humans**, regardless of **race**, **gender** or **sexuality**.

- **Mahayana Buddhists** believe that **all humans** are born with the **nature of the Buddha** within them. This **Buddha-nature** means that **everyone** (regardless of race, gender or sexuality) can become **enlightened** if they live the right **kind of life.**

- The **Dalai Lama** teaches that all humans are **equal** because we all experience **suffering**. He encourages Buddhists to show **tolerance** and **kindness** to everyone, including those from **other religions**.

Attitudes to Equality

Traditionally, religions have supported different gender roles

Christian attitudes to gender equality have shifted

For more on this, see p.45.

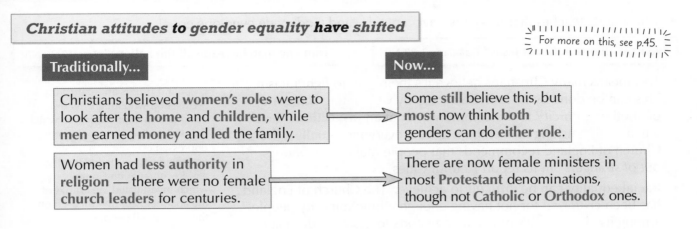

Traditionally...

Christians believed **women's roles** were to look after the **home** and **children**, while **men** earned **money** and **led** the family.

Women had **less authority** in **religion** — there were no female **church leaders** for centuries.

Now...

Some **still** believe this, but **most** now think **both** genders can do **either role**.

There are now female ministers in most **Protestant** denominations, though not **Catholic** or **Orthodox** ones.

Buddhist views on gender roles are still divided

Teachings about **gender equality** are **inconsistent** within Buddhism. Buddhists' views on gender roles tend to reflect the **culture** they live in:

The **Sigalovada Sutta** provides guidance on the different **roles** of men and women within the **family**. Men are described as **providers** and women **run the household**, but both roles are seen as **equally important**.

The **Lotus Sutra** teaches that both men and women can become **enlightened**.

> **"If there are good men or good women who, on hearing... the Lotus Sutra of the Wonderful Law, believe and revere it with pure hearts and harbour no doubts or perplexities, they will never fall into hell..."** *Lotus Sutra, Devadatta*

Some Buddhists believe that a woman must be **reborn as a man** in order to achieve enlightenment. These Buddhists use this to argue that women should **not** be ordained as **nuns**.

The **Buddha** initially said that women could **not** become **nuns**, but his **aunt** convinced him to change his mind. This was a **radical decision** because during the time in which the Buddha was alive, women were seen as **subservient** to men.

So, now you know these pages off by heart and backwards...

EXAM QUESTION

...try this exam question. If you don't feel you know the topic well enough, read the pages again. 'Men and women should have the same roles within religion.' *Evaluate this statement, making sure you refer to religious views which support and disagree with it, and give a conclusion.* [12]

| Christianity & Buddhism | **Attitudes to Equality** |

Christian *and* Buddhist *teachings oppose racism*

- Christianity teaches that racism is unacceptable, and God made everyone equal.

| "you are all one in Christ Jesus" *Galatians 3:28 NIV* | "From one man he made all the nations" *Acts 17:26 NIV* |

- This means many Christians believe it's their duty to fight racism. This can be done by an individual, e.g. by welcoming someone of another ethnicity to the community, or at an institutional level, e.g. a church asking its members to treat everyone equally. The Church of England recommends that people make "*neighbours out of strangers*" in its report Faithful Cities.
- Racial equality can be difficult to achieve. The Church of England has been criticised for not having enough ethnic minority people among its clergy — it's now making efforts to increase diversity.

> Desmond Tutu is an Anglican archbishop who fought against apartheid in South Africa, in which the white minority population oppressed everyone else. After apartheid ended, he led the Truth and Reconciliation Commission, which investigated the crimes of the apartheid era and focused on the unity of all people.

- Buddhists believe that all humans experience suffering because of ignorance, greed and hate. Feelings of hatred or dislike towards others should be let go of and replaced with feelings of loving kindness towards all humans.
- If a Buddhist sees themselves as superior to others then they are being ignorant. There is no fixed self (anatta), so no person can be better than another person. Wanting to be superior is a craving for the self and leads to suffering.
- Despite these views, there are examples of Buddhists being racist. Most Buddhists' views on racism reflect the society they live in.

> The Dalai Lama's first commitment is to promote the values of tolerance and compassion. He teaches that Buddhists should be welcoming towards all humans, regardless of race.

> "we are all basically the same human beings. We all seek happiness and try to avoid suffering." *Dalai Lama*

Homosexuality is controversial in Christianity

Views SUPPORTING homosexuality	Views AGAINST homosexuality
- Many Christians focus on loving their neighbour and therefore accept homosexuality. - Many individual members of the Church of England and the Catholic Church disagree with their Churches' stances on homosexuality.	- Homosexuality is a sin, and is forbidden by Bible teachings such as 1 Corinthians 6:9-10. - Church of England bishops issued a report in 2017 saying they wouldn't change the Church's definition of marriage as being between one man and one woman (Canon B30). - The Catechism of the Catholic Church 2357 says homosexual acts are "*contrary to the natural law*".

There are very few teachings about homosexuality in Buddhism

Buddhists' views on homosexuality tend to reflect the country they live in.

- Many Buddhists believe that as long as a relationship doesn't involve sexual misconduct, then it is acceptable. Some Buddhist countries have made homosexuality legal (e.g. Thailand) and many Buddhist Temples welcome homosexuals and hold blessings for same-sex marriages.
- Buddhists living in countries where same-sex marriage is illegal (e.g. Sri Lanka) are more likely to disagree with homosexuality. These Buddhists may view homosexual sex as sexual misconduct (one of the Five Moral Precepts).

Human Rights

Human rights are **moral**, **legal** and **political** rights that should give people **freedom** and **protection** worldwide.

The *United Nations* defined *human rights*

In 1948, the **United Nations** (UN) published the **Universal Declaration of Human Rights**. This **stated** how things **should** be, but meant **nothing** in a court of law. So in 1953, the Council of Europe brought into effect the **European Convention on Human Rights**.

The Universal Declaration of Human Rights

• Its aim was to lay down minimum **rights** for **every person**, in **every country**.
• It states that all human beings are born **free** and **equal** in dignity and rights.
• It also lists specific rights, e.g.:
  • the right to **life**
  • freedom from **slavery**
  • freedom from **imprisonment** or **exile** without **good reason**
  • freedom of **opinion** and **expression**
  • the right to have an **education** and to seek **work**

European Convention on Human Rights
• This is a **similar** list of rights to the UN declaration. • It's enforced by the European **Court** of Human Rights (ECHR). • These rights became part of the UK's **domestic law** in 1998, with the **Human Rights Act**.

The European Court of Human Rights. (I think.)

Most religious believers agree that all human beings should be treated **fairly** and with **respect**. This is based on a belief in **human dignity** (all human life is **valuable**, because people are created in the **image of God**) and a belief in **justice**, e.g. Christians believe that everyone should be treated **fairly**. Everyone should be **free** to **think** and to **choose** how to act (though hopefully they'll choose a good **moral** life).

Many *Christians* support *human rights*

The **Catholic Church** highlights the role of the **individual** as well as the **state** in **protecting** human rights. It says human rights aren't just defined by **states** putting them into **law**:

> **"Every member of the community has a duty ... in order that the rights of others can be satisfied and their freedoms respected."** *The Common Good and the Catholic Church's Social Teaching: 37*

Christians may find their views **contradict** others' ideas about rights. E.g. many think **women** should have the right to **abortion**, but some Christians **disagree**, believing the **foetus's** right to **life** is more **important**.

> **"You ... were called to be free. But do not use your freedom to indulge the flesh; rather, serve one another humbly in love."** *Galatians 5:13 NIV*

Buddhists *support human rights too*

- In order to become **enlightened**, a Buddhist must live a certain **type of life**. This is only possible if the person is **free to make choices** about the kind of life they live, e.g. if you're not free to express your **opinions** and **thoughts** then it's **impossible** to have **right speech**.

- Treating another human **without respect** is not the **compassionate** thing to do. Taking away another human's rights will only cause **more suffering**, and causing another human to **suffer** goes against the **First Moral Precept**.

- The **Dalai Lama** was forced into **exile** in India in 1959, after the **Tibetan uprising**, when Tibetan fighters tried to fight against Chinese occupation. During this time, many Tibetan people were killed and Buddhist monasteries were destroyed. The Dalai Lama has spent most of his life campaigning for the **freedom** of the Tibetan people.

REVISION TASK

The right to drink tea is an important part of British law...

...just kidding. Quite a good idea though. Anyway, back to business — shut the book and have a go at writing down as many of the human rights on the page as you can remember.

Freedom of Belief

You need to be able to give **contrasting** religious views on this **topic**.

The UK is a diverse, multi-faith society

- **Freedom of religion** and **belief** is a **legal** right in the UK — it gives the freedom to follow **any** or **no** religion.
- People are protected from being **discriminated** against because of their **beliefs**.
  The **beliefs** they hold as part of their religion are **protected**, e.g. religions can choose **not** to hold **same-sex marriages** in their **places of worship** if it doesn't fit with their **beliefs**.

About half of the population say they have no religious belief.

Freedom of belief is sometimes a tricky area though...

- Some people feel there isn't **enough recognition** of those who **don't** hold religious beliefs, e.g. in **religious studies** in **schools**.
- There can be a fine line between **educating** people about a **faith** and **influencing** them too much. Some people think, e.g.:

> **Religious charities** have too much influence.

> The charities aren't trying to **convert** people, just **help** them.

- Some people, including religious believers, object to the **Church of England** being the **state** church, e.g.:

> 26 **bishops** are peers in the **House of Lords**, which is **unfair** now that the country is more religiously **diverse** and many people **don't have** a religion at all.

> The UK is a **Christian country** so it's **acceptable** — it's part of the **culture**.

- A religious person saying homosexuality is **sinful** clashes with homosexual people's **right** not to be **discriminated** against and could be seen as **hate speech** (a **crime**), but **stopping** people from expressing their views **undermines** their **freedom of belief**.

- Most religious believers happily live alongside others in the UK and enjoy the **different perspectives** it gives them. The **Inter Faith Network for the UK** promotes mutual **understanding** and **combats prejudice**.
- Living in a multi-faith society can make it **harder** for some believers to **practise** their **faith** — e.g. some **Christian** festivals are UK **bank holidays** while other faiths' festivals **aren't**, making it **harder** to **celebrate**.

Many Christians think people can follow any faith

- Though many Christians think Christianity's the **true** religion, they think people have the **right** to practise **any faith**.
- Some Christians think the **only way** to reach heaven is by being Christian, so they try to **convert** people.

> *"[It's] an inalienable requirement of the dignity of man." Catechism of the Catholic Church 1747*

Buddhists show tolerance towards people of all faiths

- Buddhists try to show **loving kindness** towards all people, even if they disagree with a person's way of life.
- Buddhists do **not** see the **Dhamma** as a **set of rules** and so will not try to **convert** anyone to their faith. Instead, the Dhamma guides people on their path to **enlightenment** — it is up to each person to **choose** to follow the path.
- Tenzin Gyatso, the 14th **Dalai Lama**, is committed to encouraging **peace** between religions. For example, he has written a book with Archbishop Desmond Tutu called **"The Book of Joy"**.

> **"Despite philosophical differences between them, all major world religions have the same potential to create good human beings."** *Tenzin Gyatso, 14th Dalai Lama*

EXAM QUESTION

I can't do GCSEs — exams are against my religion...

...sorry, that won't wash. Try this exam-style question instead.

Explain two contrasting religious beliefs about freedom of belief. [5]

Social Justice

Social justice is the idea that everyone should have equal rights and opportunities.

Social justice is the idea that everyone should be treated fairly

Social justice is putting into practice the principles of human rights.

> **Working for social justice includes:**
>
> - Trying to ensure different groups of people aren't discriminated against or more disadvantaged than others. This includes discrimination on the grounds of race, gender, religion, social class, poverty, age or disability.
> - Trying to redistribute wealth so everyone can afford to live comfortably. Some members of society are very wealthy while others struggle to meet their basic needs for food, shelter, warmth, etc.

- Social justice efforts often focus on wealth, as a lack of it can deprive people of other opportunities and rights. Higher taxes for people on high incomes and free healthcare and education are ways to help.
- Many people try to work for social justice. It's an important part of Christianity too.

Christianity teaches that people should help those in need

Christians follow Jesus's teaching to "*Love your neighbour as yourself*" Mark 12:31 NIV.
The parable of the sheep and goats is often used to teach about social justice — see p.22 for more.

> Jesus was known for helping poor people and for healing the sick. In Luke 16:19-31, he teaches that people who don't help others when they're able to will be punished — the story is about a rich man who repeatedly ignores a poor man, and ends up in hell for not helping him. Jesus healed a man with leprosy by touching him, at a time when lepers were outcasts from society. Christians should therefore follow Jesus's example — by helping those who need it, they can express God's love.

The Catholic Church emphasises the importance of human dignity in social justice.

> **"[people should be allowed] to obtain what is their due, according to their nature and their vocation"** *Catechism 1928*

> This means people should be given opportunities to make the most of their lives and their abilities. Catechism 1928 also says social justice is better for everyone — it's for "*the common good*".

Buddhists try to reduce suffering in the world

It's important for Buddhists to show compassion towards the suffering of others:

> Some Buddhists do this by working for social justice in the world, e.g. by supporting the Karuna Trust, a charity that aims to end discrimination in Nepal and India.

> Many Buddhists focus on eliminating their own suffering through discovering the Four Noble Truths. They see politics as a distraction from the path to enlightenment and do not work for social justice. Instead, they might show compassion locally, e.g. many temples donate food to the poor.

Basically, everyone should help people who need it...

There are a few different teachings on this page, so as a fun test (or maybe just a test...), write down as many as you can remember without looking at the page. Don't forget to give the source.

Wealth and Poverty

How **wealth** is **used**, and how it's **distributed** among people, is a **big issue** today. For the **exam**, you need to be able to give **Christian** opinions on the **uses of wealth**, as well as views from **one other religious** tradition.

Wealth inequality *is a* big problem *today*

The **gap** between the **poorest** and **richest** people is **huge**, and **growing**. In 2017, **Oxfam** estimated that the richest **8** people in the world had **more wealth** than the poorest **half** of the world (**3.6 billion** people).

> **poverty**
> *not having enough resources (money, etc.) to meet your basic needs, e.g. food or heating*

Causes *of poverty include...*

In the UK

- low wages
- high costs (e.g. renting a house or paying for childcare)
- a lack of skills so people can't get better-paid jobs
- unemployment

> In the UK, the poorest 50% of people own 8.7% of wealth, while the richest 10% own 45%.

- **Fair pay** is an issue. Many in **poverty** have **low-paid** jobs, so they work **long hours** to try to earn enough to live on. In some **areas**, **well-paid** jobs **aren't** available. **Part-time** work's often low-paid.
- By law, people have to be paid the **National Minimum Wage**, but many people think it **isn't** enough. Over-25s must be paid the **National Living Wage**, which is a bit **higher** than the minimum wage. However, many say it still **isn't enough** to **live on** — it's not a **true** living wage.
- **Businesses** are often **reluctant** to pay people **more** as it's **expensive** for them to do so — some try to **avoid** paying even the minimum wage. Some say **increasing** wages will mean they **can't afford** to **pay** people so they would have to **cut** the number of jobs, which wouldn't help.

Worldwide

- war
- rapid population growth
- natural disasters
- exploitation

> The **Fairtrade Foundation** works to ensure people in **developing countries** are paid a **fair price** for the products they **sell** and that they have **decent working conditions**.

Finding a solution *is difficult*

- Helping to relieve poverty after a **disaster** (e.g. **war**) often involves **emergency relief** during the **disaster** and **long-term** help afterwards, e.g. rebuilding houses. It can take **years** before things get back to **normal**.
- People have a range of views on how to help those living in poverty in other situations:

> Giving **money** (e.g. benefits or donations) to people in poverty makes them too **reliant** on that money — they don't **help themselves** get out of poverty as they prefer to keep **receiving** the money.

 vs.

> People living in poverty need **financial help**, because **not** giving it to them means they might not be able to **eat** or **heat** their home.

> It's people's **own responsibility** to get out of poverty — they should work **harder** and use money more **responsibly**.

 vs.

> Poverty is a result of **many factors**, and many people do **work hard**. Society should help those who face **many issues** such as **illness**, or a **lack of skills** or **opportunities**.

> In 2016, 1 in 8 people employed in the UK were living in poverty (source Joseph Rowntree Foundation, 2016).

- **Charities** often try to help people learn **new skills** on top of giving them **money** or **food**.

> **Utilitarian ethics** say the **correct** course of action is the one which has the **largest** balance of **good** against **bad** outcomes for those involved. Utilitarians often think people with **excess wealth** should give to people with **less wealth**. But if the money could be spent on **another** cause that would have a **greater benefit** (e.g. preventing more climate change), then giving the money to people **in poverty** would be **wrong**.

Wealth and Poverty

There are other problems often linked with poverty

Excessive Interest on Loans

- People sometimes need **extra money**, e.g. to pay for something **unexpected**, or just to afford **food** until the **next payday**. One **way** of covering this is to take out a **loan**. A quick and seemingly easy way to do so is to borrow from a **money lender**, but **money lenders** often practise **usury**. People might take out **small** loans, but they soon become so **big** that they **can't repay** them.
- This was a **big** problem in the UK, so the **government** introduced some **regulations** to **limit** how much people have to **repay**. Now, people don't have to repay more than **twice** what they borrowed.

usury
lending money at rates that go up to thousands of per cent of interest

People-trafficking

- People living in poverty are often more **vulnerable** to **people-trafficking**. People are forced to work for **little** or **no** money, after they've been transferred to a **new place** (often **abroad**) by the **traffickers**.
- People are often persuaded to move **willingly** by the promise of a **better life** elsewhere, but once they get there the traffickers **force** them to work to pay back the money they **owe** for the **move**.

How money is used is important in Christianity and Buddhism

Christians believe it's important not to be **fixated** on wealth. Both Christians and Buddhists believe that it's what you **do** with your **money** that **counts**, as summarised in the table below.

"You cannot serve both God and Money."
Matthew 6:24 NIV

	CHRISTIANITY	BUDDHISM
Uses of money	• People with lots of wealth should use it to help others who are less well off. • They also try to avoid using their money in a way that harms others.	• The Buddha warned against living a life of **luxury** and being attached to **material things**. Buddhists try to live according to the **Middle Way** and only buy what they **need**. • Buddhists should act with **right intention**, which means being **selfless**. Spending money on things that might lead to **harming others** would go against this.
Ways of earning money	• Many Christians think money should only be earned in moral ways, not in ways that might harm others, such as working for arms manufacturers or running a business that pays people unfair wages.	• It is important that Buddhists earn money through **right livelihood** (not doing a job that harms others, e.g. selling harmful intoxicants).
Usury	• Usury is viewed as harming others. • The Church of England has launched an initiative to combat lenders who charge lots of interest. The Church is offering workshops to educate people about money matters, as well as promoting credit unions, which lend money at low rates of interest.	• Buddhists need to act with **right mindfulness** (being aware of all your actions and their consequences). Lending money with high interest rates causes **harm** and **suffering** to others, so Buddhists would be against this.

Both faiths work to end people-trafficking

- Religious leaders have created the Global Freedom Network. This is an organisation which aims to end slavery. It works with governments to get them to pass laws to combat slavery and people-trafficking.
- The Church of England campaigned for the Modern Slavery Act, to protect victims of people-trafficking.

Theme F — Religion, Human Rights and Social Justice

Wealth and Poverty

Charity *is important to* Christians

- Giving to charity and helping others is important to many Christians, following the teaching to *"Love your neighbour"* (Mark 12:31 NIV).
- It's important to give in a way that helps people to help themselves — the parable of the talents (Matthew 25:14-30) says those who make most of what they have are rewarded.
- Christians should give to charity as part of their faith. There are many Christian charities — see p.22.

> *"If anyone has material possessions and sees a brother or sister in need but has no pity on them, how can the love of God be in that person?"* 1 John 3:17 NIV

Checking your donation's gone to a worthy cause is a good idea...

- It's best to give donations quietly and without boasting about it:

> *"...when you give to the needy, do not announce it with trumpets..."* Matthew 6:2 NIV

For more teachings on wealth, see p.102 and 105.

- How much you give isn't important — what's important is giving as much as you can.

> Jesus taught that a poor woman giving a small amount of money she couldn't afford to lose was more important than rich people giving large sums they could easily do without.

- Over 7500 churches are involved with the Fairtrade movement.

For more on Fairtrade see p.86.

Buddhists *show* compassion *through* charitable giving

- Giving to charity is one way of showing compassion towards others when they are suffering, so it's important to many Buddhists, e.g. temples sometimes donate food that people have left as offerings for Buddha rupa (statues of the Buddha) to the poor.
- For Buddhists, charitable giving must be done with right intention. This means giving to others for selfless reasons and not because it makes you feel good.
- Mahayana Buddhists are encouraged to be generous — this is one of the Six Perfections that you need to become enlightened (see p.34).

> **Buddhist Global Relief** is a Buddhist organisation that provides aid to help people living in **poverty**. The charity also aims to **educate** and **support** people to ensure they can **earn money** and **access food** for themselves in the future, e.g. it donates to **Keep Growing Detroit** — a campaign that supports **gardeners** in creating sustainable food distribution across the city.

I hope you feel richer (in knowledge) after these pages...

Learning the names of charitable organisations and movements such as Fairtrade and the Buddhist Global Relief Fund can help you pick up marks by adding detail to your answers.

Revision Summary

Now here's the fun bit — let's see if you can remember what you've just read in the section. The questions below will give you an idea of what the exam will be like and how much you'll need to write. If you're struggling with anything, have another read of the section and give the questions another go once you've re-read it. When you're happy you can answer a question, tick it off. Keep an eye out for the questions that give you extra marks for spelling, punctuation and grammar — you'll need to check your writing thoroughly for those.

Let's start off with some straightforward 1 mark multiple choice questions.

1) Which of the following is prejudice against people who are homosexual? ☑
   a) Sexism   b) Homophobia   c) Racism   d) Heterosexuality

2) Which of the following people fought against apartheid in South Africa? ☑
   a) The Pope   b) The Dalai Lama   c) Desmond Tutu   d) Jesus

3) Which of the following means equality of rights and opportunities? ☑
   a) Social justice   b) Freedom of belief   c) Discrimination   d) Gender inequality

4) Which of the following is the principle the Fairtrade Foundation campaigns for? ☑
   a) Wealth inequality   b) Utilitarian ethics   c) Low pay   d) Fair pay

Right, now you need to write a bit. These are worth 2 marks, so give two short points.

5) Give two forms of prejudice. ☑

6) Give two examples of human rights. ☑

7) Give two religious beliefs about working for social justice. ☑

8) Give two ways religious believers are working to combat people-trafficking. ☑

Now on to 4 marks. You still need to make two points, but develop them more to get two marks for each. You need to write about the views of one or more religions.

Make sure your longer answers are clear by structuring your answer well and writing clear points.

9) Explain two similar religious beliefs about racism. ☑

10) Explain two contrasting religious beliefs about homosexuality. ☑

11) Explain two similar religious beliefs about human rights. ☑

For this question, you must refer to the main religious tradition in the UK and at least one other religious viewpoint. This question is worth 4 marks.

12) Explain two contrasting beliefs about the status of women in religion. ☐

5 marks available for these questions. For top marks, you need to refer to religious texts.

13) Explain two religious beliefs about equality. ☑

14) Explain two religious beliefs about freedom of belief. ☑

15) Explain two religious beliefs about charging interest. ☑

16) Explain two religious beliefs about giving to charity. ☑

And... the 12 mark question, which has an additional 3 marks available for spelling, grammar and punctuation. Try using the bullet points in the question to make a plan before you begin — you'll have to include everything the bullet points ask for in your answer, and a plan will help you remember it all. Have a good think about arguments for and against the statement before you begin.

17) 'A religious believer can only truly be righteous if they are poor.' ☑
    Evaluate this statement.
    Your answer should include the following:
    • religious arguments that support the statement
    • religious arguments that disagree with the statement
    • a conclusion

Have a look at the 'Do Well in Your Exam' section for help with writing essays.

The Start of Jesus's Ministry

In this section, the **numbers** in the **subheadings** give the **reference** for the Gospel extract you need to study.

John the Baptist *baptised people in the River Jordan (1:1-8)*

- Mark **doesn't** have any stories about **Jesus's birth** — he starts with the story of **John the Baptist**.
- Mark quotes from the Old Testament, where God says he will send a messenger to *"Prepare the way for the Lord"* (Mark 1:3 NIV). Mark says that **John** was this messenger, preparing for the coming Messiah.
- John baptised people in the **River Jordan** by **total immersion**.

 The **water** symbolises being **cleansed** of their sins — they had **repented** and now wanted to live **good** lives.

 The **River Jordan** was also **symbolic** to these people — in the Old Testament, the **Israelites** crossed the River Jordan to enter the **Promised Land**.

The people baptised in the river by John entered the new 'Promised Land' of **God's kingdom**.

- John predicted someone **greater** would come to **baptise** people, this time with the Holy Spirit:

> **"After me comes the one more powerful than I, the straps of whose sandals I am not worthy to stoop down and untie. I baptise you with water, but he will baptise you with the Holy Spirit."** *Mark 1:7-8 NIV*

The Old Testament prophet Joel had predicted the Holy Spirit would be present on Earth when the Messiah came (Joel 2). So John was saying the Messiah was coming — this Messiah was Jesus.

Jesus *was baptised by John and tempted by Satan (1:9-13)*

- **Jesus** was **baptised** in the River Jordan by John — this marked the **beginning** of Jesus's **ministry**. The **Holy Spirit** appeared as Jesus was being baptised and he heard a **voice** from **heaven**:

> **"...he saw heaven being torn open and the Spirit descending on him like a dove."** *Mark 1:10 NIV*

> **"You are my Son, whom I love; with you I am well pleased"** *Mark 1:11 NIV*

God's words show how important Jesus is to him — this was God giving Jesus his mission.

Baptism is still **important** to Christians **today** — it's how people are **welcomed** into the **Church** (see p.14).

- Then the Holy Spirit made Jesus go out into the **desert**:

> **"...he was in the wilderness for forty days, being tempted by Satan... angels attended him."** *Mark 1:13 NIV*

 Jesus was being tested — Satan, God's archenemy, was trying to make Jesus sin and go against God. But Jesus didn't give in to Satan, which shows his power. God's love for Jesus is demonstrated by the way he sent his messengers, the angels, to care for him.

Christians believe they also will be **tested** and **tempted**. But with **God's help**, they can **get through** it just like Jesus did. Christians remember Jesus's struggle during **Lent** (see p.19) — a period which tests their ability to **overcome temptation**.

Jesus's *titles* show how *important* he is

Mark calls Jesus *"the Messiah, the Son of God"* (Mark 1:1 NIV). Titles such as these explain his **role**.

SON OF GOD — By calling Jesus the 'Son of God', Mark means Jesus is God's special one — he has a unique relationship to God, and God gave him a unique mission. The title would have stressed Jesus's importance to 1st century Jews — it was used in the Old Testament for kings, and also for the whole nation of Israel.

MESSIAH — Messiah means 'anointed one' in Hebrew (Mark also uses 'Christ', which is the Greek translation). It also used to be given to the kings of Israel. It later came to mean a heavenly figure who would come to save the Jews from their enemies — Mark believed Jesus was this saviour. The Messiah was often expected as a military figure, but since Jesus wasn't, he didn't specifically use the term for himself (see p.94).

Don't mix up John the Baptist and John the disciple...

This section covers the Gospel of Mark in depth, and for the exam you'll need to know the key passages like the back of your hand. So get a cup of tea, sit down and read through them all.

Jesus's Miracles

At the start of Jesus's ministry, he performed many **miracles** as he travelled around teaching.

Jesus *forgave* and *healed* a paralysed man (2:1-12)

- When Jesus was teaching in a **crowded house**, some men carried a **paralysed man** to him. Because there were so many people, there was no way in, so they had to find an **alternative**:

> **"...they made an opening in the roof above Jesus... and then lowered the mat the man was lying on. When Jesus saw their faith, he said to the paralysed man, 'Son, your sins are forgiven'. "** *Mark 2:4-5 NIV*

Jesus was impressed by their strong faith, but didn't immediately heal the man — he first forgave his sins.

- There were people there who were **shocked** by what Jesus did:

> **"Why does this fellow talk like that? He's blaspheming! Who can forgive sins but God alone?"** *Mark 2:7 NIV*

They believed that only God could forgive sins — Jesus was falsely claiming God's authority.

- Jesus then **healed** the man, who was able to **walk** out of the room.
- The people *"praised God, saying, 'We have never seen anything like this!' "* (Mark 2:12 NIV). They realised that **Jesus's power** must have come from **God**.

The story shows **modern Christians** that they must put their **faith** in **Jesus's power**. By demonstrating his **power** through **healing**, Jesus showed he also must be **powerful** enough to **forgive sins**. But to him, forgiving sins was more **important**.

> **"But I want you to know that the Son of Man has authority on earth to forgive sins."** *Mark 2:10 NIV*

Christians have a *range of views* on the *meaning of this story*

Some believe the story may be understood **literally**, whereas others think it's **symbolic**:

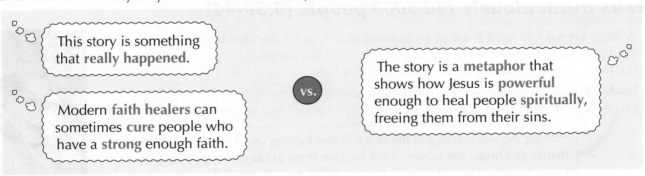

This story is something that **really happened**.

Modern **faith healers** can sometimes **cure** people who have a **strong** enough faith.

vs.

The story is a **metaphor** that shows how Jesus is **powerful** enough to heal people **spiritually**, freeing them from their sins.

Jesus uses the title 'Son of Man' in this passage

- The 'Son of Man' is a title that Jesus often uses when referring to **himself**.
- There are **various interpretations** of what the title means:

Daniel 7:13-14 talks about the Son of Man as a powerful, heavenly figure.

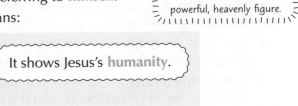

In Jesus's language, **Aramaic**, it was the normal way of talking about **yourself**, like using 'I'.

It shows Jesus's **humanity**.

Jesus's Miracles

Jesus brought a girl back to life (5:21-24 and 5:35-43)

- **Jairus**, a synagogue leader, **begged** Jesus to help his **dying daughter**.

> "My little daughter is dying. Please come and put your hands on her so that she will be healed and live." *Mark 5:23 NIV*

- But the girl **died** while Jesus was on his way. However, Jesus told Jairus to have **faith**. He'd **already** shown his faith by going to Jesus, but Jesus **encouraged** even **greater faith**.

- When Jesus saw the girl:

> "He took her by the hand and said to her... 'Little girl, I say to you, get up!' " *Mark 5:41 NIV*

> The words 'little girl' are translated from a phrase in Aramaic which literally means 'little lamb', showing Jesus's care for the child.

- The girl was brought **back to life**, and began to **move** around.

- Jesus told them **not** to mention what had happened.

Jesus was rejected in his hometown (6:1-6)

- After being away from his hometown of Nazareth, Jesus **returned** in his new role and started teaching in the synagogue.

- But the people there knew him as their carpenter, the son of Mary. They **didn't believe** he could be God's chosen one.

- Jesus said:

> "He could not do any miracles there, except lay his hands on a few people who were ill and heal them. He was amazed at their lack of faith." *Mark 6:5-6 NIV*

> "A prophet is not without honour except in his own town, among his relatives and in his own home." *Mark 6:4 NIV*

> Jesus previously said the disciples were his true relatives.

> Many Christians were (and sometimes still are) **misunderstood** and **rejected** by their **families**. They can **take heart** from the fact that it happened to **Jesus** too.

Jesus miraculously fed 5000 people (6:30-44)

- A **large crowd** followed Jesus to an isolated place, so he decided to **teach** them. As it got late, Jesus instructed his **disciples** to **feed** the people, but they only had **five loaves** of bread and **two fish**.

- Jesus manages to make the little food they have feed **everyone** — there were at least **5000 people** there but there was still lots **left over**.

> "Taking the five loaves and the two fish and looking up to heaven, he gave thanks and broke the loaves. Then he gave them to his disciples to distribute to the people. He also divided the two fish among them all." *Mark 6:41 NIV*

This miracle is important for many reasons:

- It would have reminded **1st century Jews** of the Old Testament story where God fed the **Israelites** on miraculous manna (bread) while they were with **Moses** in the **wilderness**.

- For Christians today, it's a **reminder** of how Jesus also broke bread at the **Last Supper** — Christians are **fed spiritually** by Jesus when they remember this at the **Eucharist** (see p.97).

- It also reminds them to have **faith** that God will **look after** them. He can deal with **big problems** and do great things with the **small offerings** that they make in their lives.

- The story appears in **all four Gospels** — Christians think this makes it likely that it's **true**.

Jesus's Miracles

Jesus restored sight to a blind man (10:46-52)

- **Jesus** and his **followers** came across **Bartimaeus**, a blind man, **begging** at the side of the road.

- He called out *"Jesus, Son of David, have mercy on me!"* (Mark 10:47 NIV) and told Jesus he wanted to be able to **see**. Jesus **healed** him:

> **" 'Go... your faith has healed you.' Immediately he received his sight and followed Jesus along the road"** *Mark 10:52 NIV*

- Bartimaeus **threw** away his **cloak** before going to Jesus. He would have used it to **catch coins** that people tossed to him, so he **abandoned** his means of **livelihood** to **follow** Jesus, just like the **other disciples**.

This reminds Christians today that they should **focus** more on their **faith** than on worldly goods.

Many Christians interpret this story as meaning that they're **spiritually blind** without Jesus, but if they have **faith** and **follow** him, their **eyes** will be **opened** to how they should **live** their lives.

- The title '**Son of David**' was used in this story.
- David was the **greatest** of the **kings** of Israel in the **Old Testament**, so people who used this title saw Jesus as a new king who would **rule justly**, like David did.
- Also, the **Messiah** was **prophesied** to be David's **descendant**, so by using this title, people **acknowledge** Jesus as the Messiah.

This is the last miracle in Mark's Gospel before Jesus's crucifixion in Jerusalem.

The miracle stories tell us a lot about Jesus

- The **miracles** in Mark's Gospel show how Jesus had **God's power**. They also show his **compassion** for people who were suffering or in need.

- Although Mark focuses on **Jesus's actions** in these stories, they also show Jesus as a **popular teacher**. Mark portrays how Jesus **travelled** around teaching, usually attracting **huge crowds**.

The miracle stories can be interpreted in different ways

By Christians...

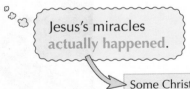

Jesus's miracles **actually happened**.

They're **metaphors** that **symbolise** a **spiritual truth**.

Some Christians accept **both** these meanings.

And by non-religious people...

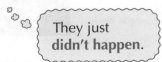

They just **didn't happen**.

There are ways to **explain** the events **rationally** using **science**.

REVISION TASK

Learn this and you won't need a miracle to pass the exam...

These stories show Christians how they should follow Jesus and have faith in their everyday lives. See if you can jot down a quick summary of each miracle, and why they're important for modern-day Christians.

Theme G — St Mark's Gospel: the Life of Jesus

The Later Ministry of Jesus

It's not until the second half of Mark's Gospel that Jesus is recognised as the Messiah.

Jesus was declared the Messiah and predicted his death (8:27-33)

This is an important turning point in Mark's Gospel. Jesus's ministry in Galilee had finished, and he was starting to move towards Jerusalem, where he knew he would die.

- Jesus and his disciples were travelling near the town Caesarea Philippi when he asked them, "*Who do people say I am?*". They told him: "*Some say John the Baptist; others say Elijah; and still others, one of the prophets*" (Mark 8:27-28 NIV).

  > John the Baptist had been executed, so some people thought he'd come back from the dead in Jesus.

- So far, no-one had said that Jesus was the Messiah. But when Jesus asked his disciples who he was, Peter replied: "*You are the Messiah*" (Mark 8:29 NIV).

- But Peter had misunderstood Jesus's real mission — he may have thought the Messiah would be a political or military figure (see p.90).

- Jesus then tells them about how he would suffer and die — but would come back to life:

  > "**...the Son of Man must suffer many things and be rejected by the elders, the chief priests and the teachers of the law... he must be killed and after three days rise again.**" *Mark 8:31 NIV*

- Peter told him off. He thought it was impossible for the Messiah to die, so Jesus must be wrong.

- Jesus replied: " '*Get behind me, Satan! ... You do not have in mind the concerns of God, but merely human concerns*' " (Mark 8:33 NIV).

  > Jesus was criticising Peter for trying to tempt him away from his true mission from God, just as Satan had tempted Jesus in the wilderness. However, God's plan for salvation involved Jesus being crucified.

Jesus's true nature was shown to the disciples (9:2-9)

- Jesus went up a mountain with Peter, James and John — the three disciples he was closest to. Then, his appearance changed:

  > "**His clothes became dazzling white... And there appeared before them Elijah and Moses, who were talking with Jesus.**" *Mark 9:3-4 NIV*

  > Elijah and Moses were two of the greatest figures of the Old Testament. Moses gave Jews the Law and Elijah was the greatest of the Prophets. The way that they appeared with Jesus showed he was the Messiah in the Old Testament prophecies.

- This is called 'the transfiguration'. The disciples were shown the true divine nature behind Jesus's normal appearance.

- God spoke:

  > "**...a cloud appeared and covered them, and a voice came from the cloud: 'This is my son, whom I love. Listen to him!'**" *Mark 9:7 NIV*

  > This demonstrates how important Jesus's words were.

- On the way down, Jesus forbade them to speak about it until he had come back from the dead.

- The story reveals just how important Jesus was, and the power that God had given him.

It's time to show your true nature as a dedicated student...

Give two reasons why Peter was angry when Jesus told the disciples he would die. [2]

Theme G — St Mark's Gospel: the Life of Jesus

The Later Ministry of Jesus

The *Messianic Secret* is a big part of Mark's Gospel

- Jesus told his disciples **not** to **tell** anyone that he was the **Messiah**. The real **nature** of Jesus's **messiahship** is only truly **understood** after the resurrection — this is the **Messianic Secret** in Mark.
- This has many parts:

> For example, Jesus told people **not** to talk about the **miracles** he performed, and his teachings in the form of parables could be **difficult** to **understand** (see p.101-102).

- He may have wanted to keep his messiahship a **secret** in case it was **misunderstood**.

> Although Jesus tried to keep it a secret, by the time he got to Jerusalem, people were calling him the Messiah.

Jesus predicted his death and resurrection again (10:32-34)

- While going to **Jerusalem**, Jesus **again** told the disciples he would be **killed**, but would **rise** from the **grave**.
- This was the **third time** he predicted his death — he gave **more detail** than before:

> "...the Son of Man will be delivered over to the chief priests and the teachers of the law. They will condemn him to death and will hand him over to the Gentiles, who will mock him and spit on him, flog him and kill him. Three days later he will rise." *Mark 10:33-34 NIV*

> The Gentiles were the **Romans** — the Jews couldn't **execute** people because the Romans **ruled** over them, so they would have to **give** Jesus to the Romans.

> This was one of his 'passion predictions' — Jesus's suffering and death are called the 'passion'.

- The things Jesus predicted later **happened** (see p.97-99). Mark presents the events as the **fulfilment** of Jesus's **prophecy**, and as part of the **divine plan**.
- The **crucifixion** came as a devastating **shock** to the disciples. But eventually they came to understand that it was an **essential** part of **God's plan**, not a defeat. Mark shows that Jesus **understood** this **in advance** and continued to Jerusalem despite **knowing** what awaited him.

It's no secret that Jesus's ministry could be in the exam...

Jesus did a lot during his time on Earth, so it might be easy to get it all jumbled up. Try drawing a timeline of the events described over the last few pages, to help you remember what happened and when. Add some notes on the main points of each story, and you'll be set for the exam.

The Later Ministry of Jesus

Jesus told his disciples about serving others (10:35-45)

- **James** and **John** asked to sit on Jesus's **right** and **left sides** when he returned to **heaven** in **glory**. They wanted to be the **closest** to Jesus, and the **most important**.

- Jesus asked if they would be willing to go through the **trials** he'd suffer. They said yes. Jesus said they'd **suffer**, but the **places** by his side were **decided by God**.

> **"Can you drink the cup I drink..."**
> *Mark 10:38 NIV*

- The **other disciples** were **angry** that James and John wanted to be more important than them. Jesus said:

> **"...whoever wants to become great among you must be your servant, and whoever wants to be first must be slave of all. For even the Son of Man did not come to be served, but to serve, and to give his life as a ransom for many."** *Mark 10:43-45 NIV*

Only people who were humble and served others on Earth would be rewarded in heaven. Jesus would later serve humanity by dying so that they would be reconciled with God (see p.11).

Many Christians try to **serve** others, e.g. through their **job** or by **dedicating** themselves to the **Church**.

Jesus entered Jerusalem as a new king (11:1-11)

- Jesus and his disciples were getting **near** to **Jerusalem** — the **holy city** where **David** and the other kings had reigned. Jesus told two disciples to bring him a young **donkey** (a colt), which Jesus rode.

- In the Old Testament, the Messiah was predicted to enter Jerusalem on a **donkey** (Zechariah 9:9).
- Riding in on a donkey showed Jesus's **humility** and **peaceful** nature, something Christians should try to **follow**.

- Some people laid **cloaks** and **branches** across Jesus's path, which showed how **respected** he was.

- As he rode into Jerusalem, they cried:

> **"Hosanna! Blessed is he who comes in the name of the Lord! Blessed is the coming kingdom of our father David!"** (Mark 11:9-10 NIV).

Hosanna means 'save now' — the people of Jerusalem believed that Jesus was the Messiah, and was there to help them.

- Jesus is celebrated as David's successor — the new **messianic king**. This follows straight after Bartimaeus called him 'Son of David' (see p.93).

Christians remember this event on **Palm Sunday**, named after the branches people used. They're reminded of how Jesus was **proclaimed** as the **saviour**, and also of his **humility**. But Christians today **know** how the crowd soon **turned against** Jesus. They must be **careful** to keep their **faith** in him.

Serving others is important, so here's something for you...

See if you can summarise the events that took place in the later stages of Jesus's ministry. Extra points if you can back them up with specific references to Mark's Gospel.

The Final Days in Jerusalem

Jesus had arrived in **Jerusalem**, and he knew that this was where he would be **betrayed** by one of his disciples.

Jesus ate with his disciples at the Last Supper (14:12-26)

- Jesus and the disciples ate the **Passover meal** together — this is known as the **Last Supper**.

> Passover is the Jewish festival that remembers the Jews' escape from slavery in Egypt. Christians believe that the death of Jesus also rescues people from sin and death.

- At the meal, Jesus predicted that one of the disciples would **betray** him. They all denied it.

> **"Truly I tell you, one of you will betray me — one who is eating with me"** Mark 14:18 NIV

- He **divided** up some **bread** and passed it to **everyone**, saying, "*Take it; this is my body*" (Mark 14:22 NIV). Then he **passed** around a cup of **wine**, saying "*This is my blood of the covenant, which is poured out for many*" (Mark 14:24 NIV).

- It reflected how Jesus's **body** would be broken, like the bread, and his **blood** shed at the **crucifixion**.
- 'Covenant' referred to the **agreement** God made with the **Jews** in the **Old Testament**.
- Jesus was saying that his life and death created a **new relationship** with God.

- Jesus also said, "*...I will not drink again from the fruit of the vine until that day when I drink it new in the kingdom of God*" (Mark 14:25 NIV). He knew that his **death** was **near**.

Jesus's actions are still very important to Christians today — they re-enact them in the Eucharist. But there are different beliefs about what Jesus's words meant.
- Some believe the **bread** and **wine** had **literally** become his **body** and **blood**, whereas others think he meant that they just **represented** them.
- This is why the **Eucharist** is celebrated in different ways — read the **third section of p.14** for more about this.

Jesus was arrested in the Garden of Gethsemane (14:32-52)

- Jesus told the disciples to **keep watch** as he **prayed** in the **Garden of Gethsemane**, but they fell asleep.
- Jesus asked **God** if he could **avoid** what was coming, but then he **submitted** to **God's will**.

> **"Abba, Father... everything is possible for you. Take this cup from me. Yet not what I will, but what you will."** Mark 14:36 NIV

Jesus was afraid to go through with the suffering ahead — this shows that he was a real human being. But his obedience to God is an example for Christians. Early Christians followed his example in trusting God, even when persecuted.

- Then **Judas** (one of the disciples) arrived with the chief priests' **armed men**. He **betrayed** Jesus with a **kiss**.

> **"The one I kiss is the man; arrest him and lead him away under guard"** Mark 14:44 NIV

Jesus was placed under **arrest** by the men.

- One of the **disciples** "*drew his sword and struck the servant of the high priest, cutting off his ear*" (Mark 14:47 NIV). Then, the disciples all **ran away**.
- Jesus **questioned** why he was being **captured** — he asked if they thought he was leading a **rebellion**, which he **wasn't**. But he said, "*the Scriptures must be fulfilled*" (Mark 14:49 NIV).

This was just the beginning of Jesus's suffering...

Give two reasons why Jesus's words and actions in the Garden of Gethsemane are important. [2]

The Final Days in Jerusalem

Jesus was *tried* by the *Jewish authorities (14:53, 57-65)*

- Jesus was tried before the Jewish high priest.
- The high priest asked him: *"Are you the Messiah, the Son of the Blessed One?"* (Mark 14:61 NIV).
- Jesus replied *"I am... And you will see the Son of Man sitting at the right hand of the Mighty One and coming on the clouds of heaven"* (Mark 14:62 NIV).
- Witnesses gave false evidence against him, and their stories didn't agree. But Jesus was found guilty of blasphemy (because they believed he was falsely claiming to be divine) — a crime carrying the death penalty. He had to be handed to the Romans for his punishment.

> **blasphemy**
> *insulting or showing disrespect to God or other aspects of religion*

Jesus was *sentenced to death* by the *Roman governor (15:1-15)*

- Jesus was tried before the **Roman governor**, **Pilate**, the next day. Blasphemy **wasn't** a crime to the Romans, but he could have been a **political** threat. Pilate asked Jesus if he was the **king of the Jews**. He answered *"You have said so"* (Mark 15:2 NIV). He **didn't defend** himself — he **submitted** to God's plan.
- Pilate **realised** Jesus wasn't really a threat — the priests had handed him over because they **didn't** like him. Since a prisoner was released every **Passover**, Pilate offered to **release** Jesus.
- But the chief priests got the **people** to ask for **Barabbas**, a murderer, instead. When Pilate asked about Jesus they said *"Crucify him!"* (Mark 15:13 NIV). So Jesus was **flogged** and sent to be **crucified**.

Jesus was *crucified*, *died* and was *buried (15:21-47)*

- **Simon of Cyrene** was made to **carry** Jesus's **cross** to **Golgotha** ('the place of the skull').

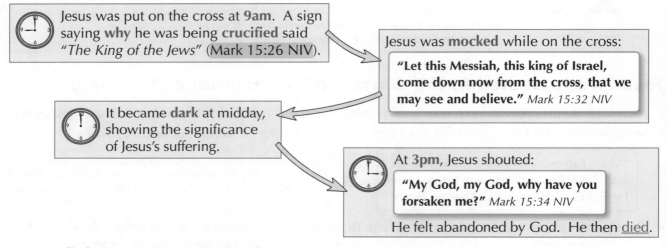

Jesus was put on the cross at **9am**. A sign saying **why** he was being **crucified** said *"The King of the Jews"* (Mark 15:26 NIV).

Jesus was **mocked** while on the cross:

"Let this Messiah, this king of Israel, come down now from the cross, that we may see and believe." *Mark 15:32 NIV*

It became **dark** at midday, showing the significance of Jesus's suffering.

At **3pm**, Jesus shouted:

"My God, my God, why have you forsaken me?" *Mark 15:34 NIV*

He felt abandoned by God. He then <u>died</u>.

- As Jesus **died**, the temple **curtain ripped** in two.

This curtain hid the Holy of Holies — a special room inside the temple where God was believed to be present, and only the high priest could enter. This showed that everyone now had access to God.

- The Roman **soldier** who saw Jesus die said *"Surely this man was the Son of God!"* (Mark 15:39 NIV). He **recognised** who Jesus was, but the Jewish leaders **didn't**.
- **Joseph of Arimathea** was given Jesus's **body** by Pilate. He *"bought some linen cloth, took down the body, wrapped it in the linen, and placed it in a tomb cut out of rock"* (Mark 15:46 NIV).

> Many Christians believe that Jesus's death **saved mankind** and **repaired** the **relationship** with God. But there are **various views** about the crucifixion — read the **first section of** p.11 for more detail.

The Final Days in Jerusalem

Jesus's tomb was found empty (16:1-8)

- Three women went to Jesus's tomb on **Sunday morning**, but they found the stone **rolled back** and the tomb **empty**. There they saw a **man** in white (an **angel**). He told them "*He has risen! He is not here*" (Mark 16:6 NIV). He told them to tell the disciples that Jesus would meet them in **Galilee**.

- The women left the tomb, **frightened** and **confused** by what they saw. They **didn't** tell anyone about it.

- Some early Bibles **finish** the story **here**, but later copies added **reports** of encounters with the **risen Jesus**.

- The resurrection turned **despair** to **hope** for the disciples. Everything **hadn't** gone **wrong** — the crucifixion was part of **God's plan**.

> The resurrection is **important** to Christians for many reasons — read the box in the **middle of p.10**. It shows that **Jesus** really is **God's son**. It would also have given persecuted early Christians hope that there was something else beyond their suffering.

HOWEVER...

Many people believe the resurrection is scientifically impossible — they explain the empty tomb in other ways. But those who believe in the resurrection have arguments against these explanations.

The women got the **wrong tomb**.	**vs.**	**Mark 15:47** says Mary Magdalene **saw** the **tomb** where Joseph laid Jesus's body.
Jesus **wasn't** really **dead**.	**vs.**	At Pilate's request, a **soldier confirmed** he had died (**Mark 15:44-45**).
The disciples **stole** the **body**.	**vs.**	Why would the **terrified** disciples **risk** their **lives** for a dead body?

Luckily for you, there's more Mark in the next section...

Not only do you need to know what happened in the last few days of Jesus's life, but you also need to know what these events can mean to different Christians. Some things, like what Jesus says at the Last Supper, are interpreted in various ways, so make sure you learn the differences.

EXAM TIP

Revision Summary

That was quite a lot to take in there, so now try out these **questions** to see what you're **comfortable** with and what needs a **bit more work**. They're like the ones you'll be asked in the actual **exam**.

If there's anything you **can't** answer, **go back** through the section and have **another go** when you've re-read it. For some questions — you'll be told which ones — there are **extra marks** for **spelling**, **punctuation** and **grammar**, so check your writing carefully.

Nice and easy to start off with — some 1 mark multiple choice questions.

1) Which one of the following is <u>not</u> a title given to Jesus in Mark's Gospel?
   a) Son of God   b) Messiah   c) Son of Man   d) Prophet

2) Which of these men did Jesus help to see?
   a) Bartimaeus   b) Jairus   c) Elijah   d) Pilate

3) Which of the disciples said that Jesus was the Messiah at Caesarea Philippi?
   a) James   b) John   c) Peter   d) Judas

4) At which of these places was Jesus crucified?
   a) Nazareth   b) Gethsemane   c) Golgotha   d) Jericho

Let's up the ante. 2 marks available per question, 2 short points to get them.

5) Give two examples of healing miracles performed by Jesus.

6) Give two reasons why Christians believe they should serve others.

7) Give two ways that Jesus kept his messiahship a secret.

8) Give two predictions Jesus made at the Last Supper.

Now on to some 4 mark questions. For full marks, you'll need to further explain your points.

9) Explain two contrasting views about the meaning of the title 'Messiah'.

10) Explain two contrasting views about the meaning of the title 'Son of Man'.

11) Explain two contrasting views about how Jesus's death saved mankind.

12) Explain two contrasting views about why Jesus's tomb was found empty.

> For the 4 and 5 mark questions, make sure your answer is well-organised so it's clear for the examiner.

5 marks for these questions. You'll have to include references to Mark's Gospel too — this could be by quoting, paraphrasing or referring to a chapter and verse.

13) Explain two ways in which the story of Jesus's baptism is important for Christians today.

14) Explain two ways in which the miracle of feeding the 5000 is important for Christians today.

15) Explain two ways in which Jesus's crucifixion is important for Christians today.

16) Explain two ways in which the resurrection is important for Christians today.

Everyone's favourite part of the exam — the 12 mark question (with an extra 3 marks for SPaG). You'll get a handy list of bullet points telling you what you must put in your answer, so use them to map out a plan. Jot down all the possible arguments for and against — that way you won't forget any.

17) 'The miracles Jesus performed didn't actually happen — they were metaphors.'
    Evaluate this statement.
    Your answer should include the following:
    • references to Mark's Gospel
    • religious arguments that support the statement
    • religious arguments that disagree with the statement
    • a conclusion
    You can also include non-religious points of view in your answer.

> 'References to Mark's Gospel' means either quotations, paraphrasing or chapter and verse references.

Theme G — St Mark's Gospel: the Life of Jesus

The Kingdom of God

This section looks at Mark's Gospel and the **kingdom of God**, and 1st century **society**, **faith** and **discipleship**.

The *Kingdom of God* can have *different meanings*

The kingdom of God is the **time** and **place** where **God rules**.
People will follow **God's will** and **live** according to it:

> "your kingdom come, your will be done, on earth as it is in heaven" *Matthew 6:10 NIV* ⟶ This is from the **Lord's Prayer**.

- It was a **central** part of **Jesus's preaching**. He explained that:

> "The time has come... The kingdom of God has come near. Repent and believe the good news!" *Mark 1:15 NIV*

- 'Kingdom of God' refers to **different times** and **places** in different passages of the Gospel:

The kingdom might exist as a state of being within the hearts and minds of individuals, or in the love and care shown within the community of believers. This applies both to Jesus's disciples and Christians now.	It can also refer to a physical kingdom in the future — God will establish a kingdom throughout the world, when Jesus returns in the Second Coming and the Last Judgement takes place (see p.8). Some think it may have already partly arrived in Jesus's healings and exorcisms (they show God's rule over sin and evil) but is still to arrive fully.

- Jesus explained what the kingdom of God is like by using **parables**.

> **parable**
> *a story about everyday life which contains a message about spiritual truth*

Parable of the *sower* — people *react differently* (4:1-9, 14-20)

Jesus told a story about a **farmer** who went to **sow seeds** in his field, and the seeds **fell** in **different places**. What happens to the seeds represents how people **respond differently** to Jesus's **teaching**.

 Some of the seed *"fell along the path, and the birds came and ate it up"* (Mark 4:4 NIV). The birds are a metaphor for **Satan** — it's **easy** for him to make people **forget** Jesus's teaching. These people **hear** the teaching, but **don't act** on it.

 Some fell where there was **little soil**. Although they quickly **grew**, they **died** from exposure to the hot **sun**: *"they withered because they had no root"* (Mark 4:6 NIV). This represents people who **accept** Jesus's message, but **give up** when things get **difficult**.

 Some *"fell among thorns, which grew up and choked the plants, so that they did not bear grain"* (Mark 4:7 NIV). These symbolise people who **accept** Jesus's message, but get **distracted** by other things, e.g. **money** and **greed**.

 Some seed *"fell on good soil. It came up, grew and produced a crop..."* (Mark 4:8 NIV). This group refers to people who **understand** Jesus's teaching, and try to **live** their lives by it.

- Jesus told the disciples that *"The secret of the kingdom of God has been given to you"* (Mark 4:11 NIV).
- The parable shows that the **kingdom of God** is present through people who **follow** Jesus's **teaching**. It encourages Christians to spread Jesus's **message**, but to **accept** that people **won't** always respond.

Parable of the *growing seed* — *symbol* of the *kingdom* (4:26-29)

Jesus told people that the **kingdom of God** was like a **farmer** who sows **seed** in a field:

> "Night and day... the seed sprouts and grows, though he does not know how. All by itself the soil produces corn — first the stalk, then the ear, then the full grain in the ear. As soon as the corn is ripe, he puts the sickle to it, because the harvest has come." *Mark 4:27-29 NIV*

- The parable explains that the kingdom of God **grows** in a **mysterious way**. Christians might **not** understand **how** God is working, but they can be **confident** that he **is**.
- The **harvest** represents **judgement** at the end of time — when the kingdom of God will be **fully established**. Those who've **followed** God's ways will be **harvested** to **live** in the kingdom of God.

EXAM TIP

Parables about farming — the cream of the crop...

For all parables in this section, make sure you understand the meaning behind each one, what they meant to people back in the time of Jesus, and what they mean to Christians today.

The Kingdom of God

Jesus taught people to **focus less** on **material things** so they could be a part of the kingdom of God.

Parable of the mustard seed — the kingdom would grow (4:30-32)

Jesus explained:

> "[the kingdom of God] is like a mustard seed, which is the smallest of all seeds on earth. Yet when planted, it grows and becomes the largest of all garden plants... the birds can perch in its shade" *Mark 4:31-32 NIV*

Jesus was describing how the kingdom of God would grow. The parable portrays the kingdom as a community, rather than just individuals — it started with Jesus, but expanded to his first followers and then thousands of Christians.

Early Christians found this **encouraging**. Although there weren't many of them, it told them one day their **movement** would be **great**. **Birds** were a Jewish symbol for **Gentiles** (non-Jews), so it also encouraged them to look for **converts** in the Gentile world too.

Some **modern Christians** think the **big plant** refers to the **Church**. The Church is a large community which provides **care** and **protection** to anyone who needs it — like a large plant does to birds. Many believe it should work to **create** the kingdom of God on **Earth**.

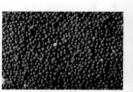

A rich man is unwilling to give up his possessions (10:17-27)

- A **rich man** asked Jesus what he must do to get **eternal life**. Jesus reminded him of the **Ten Commandments**, but the man explained that he **already** followed them.

- Jesus told him to *"sell everything you have and give to the poor, and you will have treasure in heaven. Then come, follow me"* (Mark 10:21 NIV). This may mean follow his **teachings** — or leave his home and join Jesus, **travelling** around spreading God's word.

- The man left in **despair** because he **couldn't** bear to do that.

- Jesus said to his disciples that it's very **difficult** for the **rich** to get into the **kingdom of God**:

> "It is easier for a camel to go through the eye of a needle than for someone who is rich to enter the kingdom of God." *Mark 10:25 NIV*

The 'eye' of a needle is the **small hole** which the **thread** is put through when sewing, so the saying means it's **almost impossible** for rich people to be **saved**. But Jesus does also say *"all things are possible with God"* (Mark 10:27 NIV).

'The eye of the needle' may have been a **narrow gate** in Jerusalem. Camels loaded with goods needed to be **unloaded** to **pass** through. So **rich people** have to shed their **possessions** before they can enter the **kingdom of God**, like a camel had to shed its load to enter Jerusalem.

Jesus's teaching on wealth was very surprising

Jesus's teaching on wealth surprised 1st century Jews. They believed that wealth was a sign of God's approval. But Jesus saw wealth as an obstacle to serving God fully — his disciples left their homes and possessions behind to follow him. Modern Christians interpret Jesus's teaching in a variety of ways:

> It means people shouldn't be too attached to money or possessions, but should give generously to those in need.

> It only applied to the time when Jesus lived. Giving away all your money is unrealistic now when people need money to buy even the basics. In the 1st century, people were more self-sufficient.

> Jesus's words about wealth only applied to that man — other people have different problems to overcome. The key point is that God must be first in your life — not money or anything else.

> The teaching is just wrong. If everyone gave everything away, society would collapse. It also would mean neglecting your duty to your family.

Monks and nuns take the teaching quite literally — they give up all their possessions and take a vow of poverty.

Theme H — St Mark's Gospel as a Source of Religious, Moral and Spiritual Truths

The Kingdom of God

Jesus instructed his disciples to love other people. Not just their friends — everyone.

Jesus welcomes young children despite opposition (10:13-16)

People took their children to see Jesus so he could bless them.
The disciples tried to stop it, but Jesus overruled them, saying:

> "Let the little children come to me, and do not hinder them, for the kingdom of God belongs to such as these. Truly I tell you, anyone who will not receive the kingdom of God like a little child will never enter it." *Mark 10:14-15 NIV*

He meant that the kingdom of God was for people who accepted it with childlike joy — people who are completely open to embracing new things.

The kingdom here is a present reality in the hearts and minds of individuals who apply Jesus's teaching.

This encourages modern Christians to accept Jesus's message in this way, and to treat children with love.

Love God and love other people (12:28-34)

*   The Old Testament contains hundreds of principles to follow (including the Ten Commandments).
*   A teacher of religion asked Jesus which was the greatest principle. He chose two:

1 "the Lord our God, the Lord is one. Love the Lord your God with all your heart and with all your soul and with all your mind and with all your strength." *Mark 12:29-30 NIV*

This is adapted from Deuteronomy 6:4-5. Jesus meant that God should be the thing you love most in life — nothing should be more important.

2 "Love your neighbour as yourself." *Mark 12:31 NIV*

*   This is from Leviticus 19:18. Although Jesus used the same words, in Leviticus the rule only meant love your own people — fellow Jews. Non-Jews weren't included. Jesus expanded this rule to cover all human beings.
*   It is sometimes called the Golden Rule, and this part of the Gospel is still regarded as an important rule today. It is accepted by most secular (non-religious) people.

The teacher approved of Jesus's answer. So Jesus said he was close to the kingdom of God, as he had accepted the key messages of the kingdom.

*   Many non-Christians regard Jesus as an important teacher, and a good man. Lots of modern people are inspired by his example of selfless love and forgiveness of enemies.
*   Many modern Christians agree that loving God and loving other people is the essence of Christianity. Many Christians have devoted their lives to the service of others as a consequence, e.g. Mother Teresa of Calcutta.

What if Jesus's teaching contradicts the law or government?

*   Christians believe that Jesus's character and life show what God is like. They try to obey his teachings and to live in the same way that he did.
*   Most Christians believe they should keep the laws and obey the government of the country they live in. But they believe it is right to disobey these if the laws or government are wrong.

For example, lots of Christians refused to obey the government in Nazi Germany — many hid Jews from the government so that they wouldn't be killed.

You must(ard) learn all this — it could pop up in the exam...

Create a spider diagram about the kingdom of God. Include when and where people think it might happen, what it will be like and how to get to it. Bonus points for specific Gospel references.

Theme H — St Mark's Gospel as a Source of Religious, Moral and Spiritual Truths

People Disregarded by Society

Jesus made a point of **welcoming** and **helping** those who were **excluded** from normal society.

Outcasts *were* excluded *from* society *for different reasons*

Many people were **outcasts** in 1st century Jewish society. Other people **didn't interact** with them, and they were **excluded** from **worship** — so they were **cut off** from **God** as well as from other people:

- **SINNERS** — People who deliberately **broke** the **laws** which good Jews kept were outcasts. Jews considered these laws to be **God-given**, and obeying them was **essential** to remain part of **God's people**.
- The **ILL** and **DISABLED** — These people were sometimes seen as being **punished** by God for their **sins**. Some diseases were thought to be **spread** by **physical contact**, so sufferers were **isolated** to stop others from getting **infected**. Some were thought to make the sufferer ritually **unclean**, so they couldn't join in worship. Other people couldn't **touch** them, because that made them **unclean** too.
- **GENTILES** — Parts of the **Old Testament** told Jews **not** to have any **contact** with non-Jews, and this was taught by some **rabbis** at the time of Jesus. They weren't considered to be God's people.
- The **POOR** — Very poor people **couldn't** afford to buy the **sacrifices** needed for worship at the Temple in Jerusalem. These sacrifices were **needed** to **cleanse** their sins, so they remained **sinful**.
- **TAX COLLECTORS** — They worked for the occupying **Romans**, so they were considered **traitors**. They often collected **more** than **necessary** and kept the rest for **themselves**.

Jesus welcomed outcasts — *so Christians* must too

- Jesus showed that **outcasts** were welcome in the kingdom of God. He also welcomed **women** and **children** — they were considered **less important** than **men** at the time.
- Modern Christians are inspired by his **compassion** for outcasts, and so they welcome **all** types of people. They're encouraged to **accept** and **love everyone**, whatever their gender, race, religion or past behaviour.
- This **attitude** has gradually been **built** into the **laws** of our society. **Discrimination** (treating people badly) because of their gender or race is now **illegal**.

Jesus healed *a leper and helped him back into* society *(1:40-45)*

- A **leper** asked Jesus for help. He said *"If you are willing, you can make me clean"* (Mark 1:40 NIV).
- Jesus **touched** him (making himself 'unclean') and the leper was **healed** instantly. Jesus then told him to visit a **priest** and make the **sacrifices** needed to **cleanse** a leper and **remove** his **impurity** (only a priest could declare someone free of leprosy).
- Jesus told the man to keep it a **secret** — but he told **everyone**.

leper
a person suffering from leprosy

leprosy
a skin disease that can seriously harm or even kill people. People believed it was spread by touching, so lepers were driven out of their homes.

Christians believe that they should **follow** Jesus's **teachings** and **example**.
- **Early Christians** cared for the sick during **epidemics**, and **founded** many of the first **hospitals** in Europe.
- Many **modern Christians** also care for the **sick**, despite the risks. They believe **compassion** matters more than their **own lives**, and the **best** thing they can do is **follow** Jesus's teaching.

Jesus chooses an *outcast to be a* disciple *(2:13-17)*

- **Levi** was a **tax collector** who became one of Jesus's **disciples**.
- Jesus later went to **Levi's house** to eat — other **outcasts** were also there.
  Visiting Levi's house and **eating** with him was a sign of **acceptance** of these outcasts.

"...he saw Levi... sitting at the tax collector's booth. 'Follow me,' Jesus told him, and Levi got up and followed him." Mark 2:14 NIV

- Some people **criticised** Jesus for it, but he replied: *"It is not the healthy who need a doctor, but those who are ill. I have not come to call the righteous, but sinners"* (Mark 2:17 NIV).
- Jesus showed that God values **compassion** and **helping** those in trouble **above** punishment for wrongdoing.

Theme H — St Mark's Gospel as a Source of Religious, Moral and Spiritual Truths

People Disregarded by Society

Jesus healed the daughter of a Gentile woman *(7:24-30)*

- A **Greek** (sometimes called **Syro-Phoenician**) **woman** had a **daughter** who was possessed by a **demon**. The woman asked Jesus to **heal** her.
- Jesus **refused**. He compared **Jews** and **non-Jews** to the **children** and **dogs** in a family: *"...it is not right to take the children's bread and toss it to the dogs"* (Mark 7:27 NIV). He was telling her that his **mission** was to help the Jews **before** any non-Jews.
- The woman replied: *"Lord... even the dogs under the table eat the children's crumbs"* (Mark 7:28 NIV). Because of her **humility** and **faith**, Jesus **healed** her daughter.

> Most Jews in Jesus's time had **little** to do with **Gentiles**, but there were several stories about Jesus **helping** Gentiles who approached him. Some **Gentiles** started becoming **Christians** soon after **Jesus's death**. Jesus showed that people **shouldn't** be **discriminated** against because of their **race** or **religion**.

Jesus drove a demon from a boy *(9:14-29)*

- A man's son was **possessed** by a **spirit**. It affected him **physically**: *"...it throws him to the ground. He foams at the mouth, gnashes his teeth and becomes rigid"* (Mark 9:18 NIV).
- Jesus spoke **harshly** to everyone, calling them an *"unbelieving generation"* (Mark 9:19 NIV).
- The man asked Jesus for **help**. Jesus said, *"Everything is possible for one who believes"* (Mark 9:23 NIV). But the man admitted his **faith** was **weak**: *"I do believe; help me overcome my unbelief!"* (Mark 9:24 NIV).
- Jesus told the spirit to **leave** the boy and **never** return. It **screamed**, caused the boy to **shake** and then **left**. The boy lay **still**, as if he were **dead**. But Jesus held his **hand** and helped him **up** — he was **cured**.

> Now people would recognise that the boy had **epilepsy**. But 1st century Jews — including **Mark** when he was reporting these events — didn't know the **scientific** explanation for epilepsy. Illnesses were often blamed on **demon possession** and sufferers were **shunned**.

A poor widow gave all she had to the Temple *(12:41-44)*

- People were giving **money** to the **Temple**. Some gave **lots** of money, but there was a **poor widow** who gave the **little** she had.

  Widows were very vulnerable in Jesus's society. They had no-one to protect them or provide for them — there was no help from the government.

- The **rich** donated only **spare money**, so Jesus said the **widow's gift** was **more valuable**: *"They all gave out of their wealth; but she, out of her poverty, put in everything — all she had to live on"* (Mark 12:44 NIV).

> The widow had **faith** that God would **provide** for her. This story helped **early Christians** believe that God would **provide** for them too if they had complete **faith** in him. It also shows that the **poor** are **important** to God — Christians should **help** them.

A woman anoints Jesus with expensive perfume *(14:1-9)*

- Jesus was with **Simon the Leper** when a woman tipped a jar of **expensive perfume** over Jesus's **head**.

  As well as Jesus's appreciation of this woman's actions, the story also shows Jesus's respect for lepers.

- People were **angry** with her — it was **valuable** perfume that could have been used to **help** the **poor**. But Jesus **defended** her. He said she had **prepared** his body for **burial** — this was just before his death.
- He said, *"The poor you will always have with you, and you can help them any time you want. But you will not always have me"* (Mark 14:7 NIV).

Don't disregard these stories — they're important...

Explain two ways in which St Mark's accounts of Jesus and the outcasts are important for Christians today. You should include references from Mark's Gospel. [5]

Theme H — St Mark's Gospel as a Source of Religious, Moral and Spiritual Truths

Faith and Discipleship

The disciples were Jesus's **devoted followers** during his lifetime. The **Twelve** were the most important.

Jesus first called four disciples to follow him (1:16-20)

- Simon (later called **Peter**) and **Andrew** were brothers who were **fishermen** on the Sea of Galilee. Jesus said to them:

> **"Come, follow me... and I will send you out to fish for people"** *Mark 1:17 NIV* ⟶ Jesus meant that they would **tell** people **God's message**.

- They immediately **left** their work behind and **went** with him.

- Jesus also called **James** and **John**, two more fishermen, to go with him. They *"left their father Zebedee in the boat"* (Mark 1:20 NIV) — their faith was so **strong** that they left both **work** and **family** behind.

Discipleship means learning and following

- The number of disciples grew — there were **twelve** who were especially **important** to Jesus.

> **12** Twelve was **symbolic** of the twelve **tribes** of Israel in the **Old Testament**. By choosing twelve disciples, Jesus suggested they were the **new chosen people** of God.

- 'Disciple' meant the **pupil** of a teacher, or the **apprentice** of a master craftsman, so the disciples **learned** from **Jesus**. It also meant **following** his **life** and his **example**.

> The first disciples show **modern Christians** the level of faith **expected** of them. They **sacrificed** their livelihoods and followed Jesus **without** asking any **questions**.
> - People **nowadays** might be a disciple by following a **vocation** to work for **God**, for example being a **priest**.
> - Others might carry out what Jesus **taught** people, for example by being **kind** and **helping** those in need.

Jesus told the Twelve to preach and heal (6:7-13)

- Jesus told his disciples to go out in **pairs** to **preach**, **heal** the sick and drive out **demons**.

- They took **no food**, **money** or **luggage** — they were to rely on the **hospitality** of others. If they **weren't** made **welcome** somewhere, Jesus said to **leave** and *"shake the dust off your feet as a testimony against them"* (Mark 6:11 NIV). These people had had their chance to hear the **message** — the disciples should spend **no more time** there.

- Jesus spent most of his **ministry** like this, so the disciples were **sharing** his **mission**, showing their **faith** that God would **provide** for them.

> **MISSION**
> - Early Christians were **encouraged** by this during their **missionary journeys** throughout the **Roman Empire**.
> - Mission in the 21st century is **similar** — it usually involves **practical help** as well as **preaching**. **Christian Aid** and **CAFOD** are Christian organisations which give practical help where needed in **foreign countries**.

Faith and Discipleship

Discipleship has costs as well as rewards (8:34-38 and 10:28-31)

- Jesus said his **disciples** must *"take up their cross and follow me"* (Mark 8:34 NIV).

  > He was saying they might **suffer** and **die**, as he was going to. ◁

- But anyone who showed **faith** and **gave** things **up** for Jesus would be **rewarded** both on **Earth** and in **heaven**:

  > *"...no one who has left home... for me and the gospel will fail to receive a hundred times as much in this present age... and in the age to come eternal life. But many who are first will be last, and the last first"* *Mark 10:29-31 NIV*

  - Although they'd given up family, they'd have a huge **new family** of Jesus's followers.
  - They may have been treated **badly** on Earth, but in **heaven** it'd be them, rather than their persecutors, who were **respected**.

  Early Christians would have been **comforted** by this.

- Those who opted for an easy life instead would **lose** their **future life** in the **kingdom of God**. Anyone who **disowned** him would **later** be disowned by **Jesus** on the **Day of Judgement**.

  > Modern Christians are less likely to face the same **suffering** as Jesus's early followers, but they must still be prepared to **give up** their own **wishes** and be ready for **hardship** rather than an **easy life** when they *"take up their cross"*.

Jesus heals a woman who is bleeding heavily (5:24-34)

- A woman who had been suffering from a **haemorrhage** for **12 years** approached Jesus in a crowd and **secretly** touched his **cloak**. She believed it would **heal** her and it did.

  > **haemorrhage** *excessive bleeding*

- Jesus felt **power** leave him. He **asked** who had touched him and the woman **owned up**.

- The **bleeding** meant the woman would have been seen as **unclean**, and by **touching** Jesus she would have made him **unclean** too, but that **didn't** concern him. Jesus said to her: *"Daughter, your faith has healed you. Go in peace and be freed from your suffering"* (Mark 5:34 NIV).

FAITH
- The woman in the story was **healed** because she had **faith**. Jesus often said this when he healed people.
- Faith in Mark's Gospel means **trusting God** — and **acting on** that trust.
- The woman acted by **seeking out** Jesus and **touching** him. This story shows the **importance** of **faith** for Christians.

EXAM QUESTION

The disciples spread Jesus's teachings...

...but have they taught you anything? Give this exam-style question a go and see.
Give two examples of how people in the 21st century might carry out their discipleship. [2]

Theme H — St Mark's Gospel as a Source of Religious, Moral and Spiritual Truths

Faith and Discipleship

Peter denies *he is one of Jesus's disciples (14:27-31, 66-72)*

- Just before his arrest, Jesus predicted that **all** of the disciples would **desert** him. **Peter** insisted he **wouldn't**, even if everyone else did. But Jesus said:

> **"today... before the cock crows twice you yourself will disown me three times"** *Mark 14:30 NIV*

Each disciple **swore** he would rather **die** than **desert** Jesus.

- After Jesus was **arrested**, Peter was challenged **three times** in the courtyard outside where Jesus was being held. Each time, he **denied** being one of Jesus's **disciples**.

> **"I don't know this man you're talking about."** *Mark 14:71 NIV*

- Then he heard the cock **crow twice**, and **recalled** what Jesus had said. He was very **upset**.

> **"he broke down and wept"** *Mark 14:72 NIV*

Mark considered Peter to be the **unofficial leader** of the **disciples** — he was the **first** to declare Jesus as the **Messiah**. But out of fear, even Peter **deserted** Jesus in his hour of **need**. This is a **warning** for Christians of the need for **God's help** to remain **faithful**. It **reassures** them that even the **best** Christians **fail** sometimes.

Jesus sent *his disciples out and ascended to heaven (16:14-20)*

- Jesus **appeared** to the disciples after his **resurrection**. There were only **eleven** of them — **Judas** (who had betrayed him) had **gone**.

- Jesus told them off for **not believing** the people who had seen him **alive**.

> **"he rebuked them for their lack of faith"** *Mark 16:14 NIV*

- He **commissioned** them to tell everyone about the **gospel** and to **baptise** converts.

> **"Whoever believes and is baptised will be saved, but whoever does not believe will be condemned."** *Mark 16:16 NIV*

- He predicted many **miraculous signs** would accompany their preaching. Then Jesus **ascended** to **heaven** to be with God.

- The disciples did as Jesus had **commanded** and **miraculous things** did happen — e.g. **St Paul** was **bitten** by a poisonous snake, but **survived**.
- This encourages modern Christians to **continue** the disciples' **work** — God will **protect** them while they do so. Some **Pentecostal** Churches handle **poisonous snakes** in worship as a **test of faith**.

Mark's Gospel suggests only Christians will be saved

- **Jesus's commission** to his disciples could be understood to mean that **only Christians** will be **saved**. However, verses 9-20 **weren't** included in some **original versions** of the Gospel.
- Many modern Christians **reject** this idea. They think that **other religions** can also be **paths to God**. They also respect **good people** who have **no religion**.
- **Excluding** some people could encourage **prejudice** and **discrimination**. The **rest** of Mark's Gospel is **against** both of these, and there are **laws** in the UK making discrimination **illegal** (see p.104).

(see p.104)

And that's the end of Mark's Gospel...

One of the best ways to check your understanding of something is to explain it to someone else. Try telling your friends or family about Jesus's disciples and see how much you can remember.

Revision Summary

That's the final section done and dusted, so let's see what you've **learnt**. The **questions** below
are like the ones you'll have to answer in the **exam**, so this is a good chance to **practise**.
If there's anything you **can't** answer, **go back** through the section and have **another**
go when you've re-read it. For some questions — you'll be told which ones — there
are **extra marks** for **spelling**, **punctuation** and **grammar**, so check your writing carefully.

Nice and easy to start off with — some 1 mark multiple choice questions.

1) Who did Jesus see giving all they had to the Temple?
   a) A disciple   b) A Gentile   c) A widow   d) A rich man

2) What was the occupation of Jesus's first four disciples?
   a) Tax collector   b) Soldier   c) Fisherman   d) Farmer

3) Who touched Jesus's cloak so that they would be healed?
   a) A leper   b) An epileptic boy   c) A young child   d) A bleeding woman

4) What was the name of the disciple who disowned Jesus when he was arrested?
   a) Levi   b) Peter   c) Judas   d) John

Doubling up to two marks now. All you need to do is make two short points.

5) Give two examples of parables which Jesus told about the kingdom of God.

6) Give two types of people considered outcasts in Jesus's society.

7) Give two examples of how Jesus's attitude towards outcasts is reflected in modern society.

8) Give two examples of what was expected of Jesus's disciples.

Rising to 4 marks per question. You have to develop your points to get them all.

9) Explain two contrasting beliefs about Jesus's instruction to
   "sell everything you have and give to the poor" (Mark 10:21 NIV).

10) Explain two contrasting 1st century beliefs about people with illnesses.

11) Explain two contrasting beliefs held by modern Christians about what discipleship means.

12) Explain two contrasting interpretations of Jesus's commission to his disciples.

And some more questions — this time for 5 marks. You'll need to give references from St Mark's Gospel.

13) Explain two ways in which St Mark's account of the
    parable of the sower is important for Christians today.

14) Explain two ways in which St Mark's account of Jesus's
    treatment of children is important for Christians today.

15) Explain two ways in which St Mark's account of the greatest
    commandments is important for Christians today.

16) Explain two ways in which St Mark's account of Peter's
    denial is important for Christians today.

**Drum roll please... it's time for the 12 mark question (along with an extra 3 marks for SPaG). The exam
question will have a list of points you need to make in your answer, so use it to plan things out first.
Write down arguments for and against the statement so you don't forget any while writing your answer.**

17) 'The kingdom of God has already come.'
    Evaluate this statement.
    Your answer should include the following:
    • references to Mark's Gospel
    • arguments that support the statement
    • arguments that disagree with the statement
    • a conclusion

'References to Mark's Gospel' means
either quotations, paraphrasing or
chapter and verse references.

Theme H — St Mark's Gospel as a Source of Religious, Moral and Spiritual Truths

Do Well in Your Exam

You've learnt all the **facts** — now it's time to get those **grades**.

You'll sit two exams which are worth 50% each

This information is for the <u>full course</u>. For the <u>short course</u> you'll just sit <u>one exam</u>.

You'll sit **two** exam papers: **Paper 1** is about religious **beliefs**, **teachings** and **practices**, and **Paper 2** is about the **thematic studies**.

- Both papers are **1 hour and 45 minutes** long, and they're each worth **50%** of your **overall mark**.

Paper 1

- For Paper 1, you'll be given **two booklets**, one for each of the two religions you've studied. If you've done the textual studies on **St Mark's Gospel**, you'll answer questions on **Christianity** or **Catholic Christianity**, plus **one other religion**.
- There'll be **2** questions in **each** booklet, with each **broken down** into **5** parts.
- Try to spend around **50 minutes** on each religion.

Paper 2

- In Paper 2, you need to answer the questions for the **four themes** you've studied. If you've done the textual studies on **St Mark's Gospel** (Themes G and H), you'll choose questions on the **two** religious, philosophical and ethical themes you've covered (Themes A-F), then the **two** themes on Mark's Gospel.
- There'll be **1** question **per** theme, which will be **divided** into **5** parts.
- Aim to work on **each** theme for roughly **25 minutes**.

The basics — read the questions

- **Read** the questions **carefully**. Remember to answer **all the parts** of the questions.
- Be aware of how much **time** you're using. Leave plenty of time for the long-answer questions. The more **marks** a question's worth, the **longer** you should be spending on it — for these exams, allow around **1 minute per mark**. Try to leave yourself 5 minutes at the end to **check your work**.
- Some questions will have extra marks available for **Spelling, Punctuation and Grammar** (SPaG) — there are **6 SPaG marks** available in **Paper 1** and **3 SPaG marks** in **Paper 2**. The exam paper will tell you which questions offer SPaG marks — so make your writing for these the best it can be (see p.113 for more).
- Don't use any fancy colours — write **only** in **black** ink.

1 mark questions are always multiple choice

The 1 mark questions are pretty **straightforward** — read **all** the options before you make your choice. If you're **not sure**, **guess** — you won't lose any marks.

Which of the following is the word for the Buddhist concept of impermanence?

a) Dukkha　　　　b) Anatta　　　　c) Samudaya　　　　d) Anicca

The correct answer is d) **Anicca**.

'Twas the night before the exam...

...and some people were up late, studying RS. Make sure you get a good night's rest before your exam — you won't be able to do your best if you're half asleep.

Do Well in Your Exam

There are some subtle differences between the question types, so make sure you're clear what's what.

2 mark questions just need two brief points

- The two mark questions will ask for **two** points on a particular topic. You could be asked for two **beliefs**, **examples**, **reasons**, **ways** — e.g. examples of how religious believers might act, reasons why something is important or influences believers, or ways that believers celebrate something.
- Keep your answers **short** and **to the point** — you **don't** need to write in **full sentences**.

Give two religious beliefs about divorce.

Many religious people think that divorce should be the last resort. Roman Catholics think that divorce is impossible.

Don't be tempted to **write lots**.

For the **Paper 2** questions, your points can be **general** or about a **specific religion**.

4 mark questions might ask how beliefs influence people

- The **four mark** question in the 'Beliefs' section of **Paper 1** will ask you to **explain** how a particular belief **influences** religious people.
- Make **two points**, but you'll have to **develop** them in order to get **full marks**.

Explain two ways in which believing in the Trinity influences modern Christians.

The **first** sentence here **introduces** the influence, and the **second** sentence **builds** on that point.

Christians believe that Jesus set the example for how Christians should act. By reading the Gospels, they can learn more about his life and how they should behave.
Christians believe the Holy Spirit guides them personally and the Church as a whole. They think the Spirit can help them to follow God's teachings and to live in the way God intended.

4 mark questions might ask for similar or contrasting views

- The **four mark** questions in the 'Practices' section of **Paper 1** and all of **Paper 2** will ask you to explain either two **similar** or two **contrasting** views about a topic.
- Be sure to read the **whole question**. For some 'contrasting' questions on Themes A-F, you'll be asked to write about views from **one or more religious traditions** — you can **pick** the religions.
- For others you must answer about the **main religious tradition** in the UK (**Christianity**) and **another** religious tradition. You **don't** have to write about **different religions** here — you could write about two contrasting views from **within Christianity**, e.g. from **different denominations**.

Explain two contrasting beliefs in Britain today about forgiveness.
You must refer to the main religious tradition in the UK and at least one other religious viewpoint.

Forgiveness is important to many Christians. They believe that God is always prepared to forgive sins, and Christians should accept his forgiveness and follow his example.
In Islam, some sins are seen as being so terrible that they can't be forgiven. For example, if someone commits shirk, this is considered unforgivable.

Don't let exam nerves get the better of you...

A large chunk of how well you do in the exam comes down to, well... how good you are at exams. Make sure you spend enough time practising doing exam-style questions under timed conditions. It'll pay off in the end.

Do Well in Your Exam

For 5 mark questions you must be able to refer to sacred texts

- The **five mark** questions ask you to **explain** two things, such as beliefs, teachings, ways that believers act, or reasons why something is important.

- You need to give two points and **develop** them, but for full marks you must **refer** to a **sacred text** or religious **teaching**. This could be by including a **quotation**, or by **paraphrasing** (explaining what's said in your own words). You'll need to say which text or teaching the information **comes from**. For the **Bible**, you need to say which **book** you're referring to, e.g. Genesis.

> Explain two Buddhist teachings about samsara.
> Your answer should refer to religious texts.

> There's only one mark available for referring to religious texts, so one quote or reference will do.

> Instead of giving the exact quote, you could write something like 'The Dhammapada says that if someone acts with an impure mind, suffering will follow'.

> Samsara is the cycle of rebirth, which means a person's energy continues in a new life after they die. One teaching about samsara is the idea of karma — that a person's actions can have good or bad consequences. The Dhammapada says: "If with an impure mind someone speaks or acts, suffering follows." Another teaching about samsara is that there are six realms of existence, and a person's karma will affect the realm of existence they are reborn into.

For 12 mark questions you need both sides of the argument

For the **12 mark** question, you'll need to write a **longer answer**. You'll be given a **statement** and a **list** of bullet points — these tell you what to put in your answer.

- You need to give arguments **for** and **against** the statement, so read it carefully, then make a rough list of all the **views** on each side that you can think of.

- **Plan** out your answer **before** you start writing — it needs to be **clear** and **organised** for the examiner.

- Here's an example of a **question** and **answer** from **Paper 2**:

> 'Animal experimentation should be allowed if it benefits humanity.'
> Evaluate this statement. Your answer should include the following:
> - religious arguments that support the statement
> - religious arguments that disagree with the statement
> - a conclusion
> You can also include non-religious points of view in your answer.

> The points in **Paper 1** are a bit **different**. They'll ask you to include **teachings** from the **religion** you've studied, arguments **for** and **against**, and a **conclusion**.

> Many religious believers share this point of view. They believe that animal testing is acceptable if it is for valid reasons, such as producing life-saving medicines. Testing cosmetics on animals wouldn't be considered acceptable. They also think that the animals must be treated humanely, and no unnecessary pain caused. Many religious people see themselves as stewards of the Earth, and believe they must look after animals.

> This answer starts by giving some general views that agree with the statement.

> Some religious teachings allow animal experimentation. The Catechism of the Catholic Church says that animal testing is allowed if it brings about scientific or medical advances, but the animals shouldn't be allowed to suffer.

> The second paragraph gets more specific and references religious ideas and texts.

> Some people might look at animal testing from a utilitarian point of view. If testing on animals would produce the best balance of good and bad outcomes, they would argue it is allowed.

> The third paragraph explains how ethics influence views.

> However, not all religious believers would support this view. Some people, such as the Society of Friends (Quakers), are against causing any kind of suffering to animals. They would think it's wrong to inflict pain on animals just to further our knowledge of science and medicine.

> This paragraph discusses arguments against the statement.

> You would need to include more here — this part of the answer isn't finished.

> • • • •

> I think that, although allowing animals to suffer is wrong, if the experiments could benefit humanity then they should be allowed. As for what is considered beneficial, any medical or scientific advances that could save human lives would be acceptable, but testing non-essential products such as cosmetics would not be a good enough reason to carry out animal testing. The Bible says that animals should be looked after well, so any inessential suffering in the experiment would be unacceptable.

> Finish with a conclusion — say what you think, and back it up with ideas you've discussed. These sentences should give you an idea — but you'd need to say a bit more in the real thing.

Spelling, Punctuation and Grammar

You get marks in your exams for having good **SPaG** (Spelling, Punctuation and Grammar). It might not be particularly thrilling but if you can get it right, it's **easy marks**. This page is about checking your work...

Some 12 mark questions have 3 extra marks for SPaG

- In **Paper 1**, **3 marks** are available for spelling, punctuation and grammar in the **12 mark question** on 'Beliefs', for **each** of your two religions — so that's **6 SPaG** marks available in total for Paper 1. For **Paper 2**, up to 3 SPaG marks are available for **each** 12 mark question — but it's only the **highest** SPaG mark you get across your four 12 mark questions that's counted. So that's **3 SPaG marks** available for Paper 2, meaning you could get **up to 9 marks** across the two exams just for SPaG.

- The examiner will look at your spelling, punctuation and grammar **generally**, but they'll also look at how many **technical terms** you use and how **accurately** you use them.

- Leave **5 minutes** at the end of the exam to **check your work**. That **isn't** long, so there **won't** be time to check **everything** thoroughly. Look for the **most obvious** mistakes.

- **Start** by checking the **12 mark** questions since they're the **only ones** that award SPaG marks. **Only** check the rest of your answers if you've got **time**.

My favourite kind of SPaG...

Check for common spelling mistakes

When you're writing under pressure, it's **easy** to let **spelling mistakes** creep in, but there are a few things you can watch out for:

Check for missing words as well as misspelt words.

- Look out for words which **sound the same** but **mean different things** and are **spelt differently**. Make sure you've used the correct one. For example, 'their', 'there' and 'they're':

The Bible says that wives should do what their husbands say.	There are many conditions that must be met for a war to be 'just'.	Some people might commit crime because they're living in poverty.

- **Don't** use text speak, and always write words out **in full**. For example, use '**and**' instead of '**&**' or '**+**'. **Don't** use '**etc.**' when you could give **more examples** or a **better explanation**.

- Make sure you've used the appropriate **technical terms** (like 'euthanasia', 'sacrament' or 'Bodhisattva'). If they're **spelt correctly**, it'll really **impress** the **examiner**.

Make sure your grammar and punctuation are correct

- Check you've used **capital letters**, **full stops** and **question marks** correctly.

- Make sure your writing **isn't too chatty** and doesn't use **slang words**. It should be **formal**.

- Watch out for sentences where your writing switches between **different tenses**. You should usually use **one tense** throughout your answer (don't worry if you've used a quote that's in a different tense though).

- Check that you've started a **new paragraph** every time you make a new point. It's important that your answer **isn't** just **one long block** of text.

- Watch out for tricksy little **grammar mistakes**:

  - Remember — '**it's**' (with an apostrophe) is short for '**it is**' or '**it has**'. '**Its**' (without an apostrophe) means '**belonging to it**'.

  - It's always '**should have**', not 'should of' (the same goes for 'could have' and 'would have' too).

  If you know that you **often** confuse two words, like 'it's' and 'its', **watch out** for them when you're checking your work in the exam.

Thou shalt use correct punctuation...

There's a lot of stuff to check, which is why it's really important to get to grips with it all and practise before the exam. That way you'll start to do it automatically, and make fewer errors in the first place.

Glossary and Index

The orange definitions are relevant to Christianity and Catholic Christianity.
The green ones are terms in Buddhism. The blue ones are general terms.

Glossary

Glossary and Index

Glossary and Index

Glossary